MW00653286

BREAKTHROUGH GOALS!

A COMPLETE SYSTEM FOR SETTING AND ACHIEVING YOUR GOALS

A.K. Spencer

GANESHA
MEDIA

Publisher:
Ganesha Media
2355 State St. Ste. 101
Salem, OR, 97301

Author Websites:
Akspencer.com
Linktr.ee/goalguyak
BreakthroughStrong.com
Courses.BreakthroughStrong.com

Publisher's Note: This book reflects the opinion and personal experience of the author. Nothing in this book is intended as medical or psychological advice of any kind.

Breakthrough Goals!/ A.K. Spencer. — 1st ed.
ISBN 978-1-7371774-3-2

For Mom and Dad.
I love you tons!

"If you can't, you must, and if you must, you can."
– Tony Robbins

CONTENTS

Introduction

On the path of Dharma you should be firm and fix your concentration on your goal. Otherwise you will be easily distracted.

— BHAGAVAD GITA 2:41

THIS ISN'T JUST ANOTHER BOOK ABOUT GOALS. It's that too, of course. It teaches you everything you need to know to start setting and achieving your every goal, big and small. But I prefer to think of it more as a *Choose Your Own Adventure* story, like those you read when you were a kid. Only now you are (presumably) an adult, and instead of reading about an adventure, you are going to live one. You are going to become the hero of your own story.

I want your life to be a page-turner.

It can be.

It should be.

Goals are the way to make that happen.

A bold claim, I know. But as Brian Tracy said, "Success equals goals . . . all else is commentary." I guess that makes this book an extended commentary! One I hope you will find at once exciting, challenging, and life-changing. That's what living a goal-oriented life using the method I describe in this book has done for me. And it can do the same for you.

Que back story.

THE TROPEY BUT TRUE BACKSTORY

Not so long ago I was a broke, unemployed, directionless chain-smoking drunk. I was almost sixty pounds over-weight. I was miserable, cynical, and depressed. I had very little faith in myself, and even less in the future. My worldview was dismal. My attitude, abysmal. My Spirit all but broken on the rack of anger, sorrow, fear, addiction, and too many regrets to count.

Not anymore.

Now I wake up most mornings genuinely excited about what the day may bring and all that I get to accomplish. I quit smoking (for good) and quit drinking (probably for good). I'm halfway to my ideal weight goal (glass half full). I'm my own boss with my own business (two of them, actually). I've never been in a better place financially (financial freedom here I come!). My daily routine includes exercise, mediation, prayer, writing and making art (among other disciplines). And by the time you read this I will have published my first book (let's assume it becomes a best-seller, shall we?).

I love the hell out of life. I'm grateful every day. I'm excited about the future.

I know all that may sound cheesy. In personal development books it's almost a trope to have an Introduction where the author says, "Look how my life sucked and how awesome it is now! And you *too* can go from sucky to awesome by following my simple formula!"

Well, what can I say? It's simply true. My life sucked. Now it's pretty fantastic. Key to that transformation was the system and tools I describe in this book. Them's the facts.

What's more, I also **know** that you can have the same thing. Whatever your goals, you can achieve them. Whatever life and lifestyle you aspire to, you can have it. Whatever evolution of mind, body, heart, or soul you pray for, you can experience it. And—my fear of using a tired trope be damned—this book *will* show you how.

I can make such a bold claim in all humility because very **few of the ideas contained within this book are my own**. I stand on the shoulders of giants, and you'll meet some of them in the pages that follow. I spent a over three years diving into the literature of goal setting, goal achievement, success and personal development. I tested out diverse theories and systems and through trial and error slowly separated the gold from the dross. I figured out what worked, what didn't work, and what worked okay but could work even better with a bit of tweaking.

This book is the culmination of those efforts.

The advantage for you—and it's a substantial one—is that you get to skip all the approaches I tried that *didn't* work and go straight to the fully functioning final system; you'll have a great goal plan from the starting gate.

So what makes for a genuinely great goal plan? I guess I better write a short section on that . . .

5 ELEMENTS OF A GREAT GOAL PLAN

There are five essential elements that distinguish a *great* goal plan from a merely *good* one. That's important, because the goal of your goal plan is to create a great life, not just a good life. You can't build a castle with blueprints for a cottage, after all.

These are the five elements:

1. Great Goal Plans Are Analog

There are plenty of websites and goal planning apps available now, but they're less effective than good old-fashioned pen to paper analog.

I don't know precisely why this is so, but it makes sense. Studies have shown many benefits to longhand writing, including improved cognitive functioning, creativity, and the ability to identify connections or patterns between apparently disparate things. All are essential elements to effective goal planning and achievement.

Maybe they are out there somewhere, but I've yet to find a single example of a highly successful person who relies on a digital goal planning system. They all use pen and paper. That, to me, is more telling than boring old studies on cognitive functioning that merely confirm what self-improvement literature has been saying for decades. Namely, that **if you want to achieve your goals, you must write them down**. As Brian Tracy and others have said, "A goal that's not written down is just a wish."

Where going digital *can* be effective is with time management and daily habit tracking. But that's not the same thing as goal planning, as you'll discover next.

2. A Great Goal Plan Is Goal Focused

Sounds obvious but hear me out. A great goal plan is not the same as a calendar, daily planner, or to-do list. While most goal planners will include these features, it's important to think of and treat your goals with the respect they deserve by distinguishing them from everyday tasks.

Tossing "Buy Groceries" in the same brown bag as "Build a Six-figure Home Business" cheapens your financial freedom goal. Building a profitable business is a **commitment**. We merely **do** our chores. But we **honor** our commitments. I like a sandwich as much as the next guy, but picking up a loaf of bread, bologna, lettuce, mayo, and a jar of Vlasic pickles doesn't quite rise to the level of an important goal.

From another angle, or to put it another way, the **chore** to wash your workout clothes is simply not as important as the **goal** that puts them in need of a good washing in the first place: *Working out.*

Mixing up goals and mundane tasks can also give you a false sense of accomplishment as you check off errands and everyday activities from your to-do list while procrastinating on your most important goals.

I was once very susceptible to this kind of self-defeating rationalization. "I cleaned the bathroom, organized the closet, and bought groceries. So it's no big deal that I didn't achieve today's three-hour writing goal."

Of course, it *was* a big deal because integrity is a big deal. Repeatedly breaking promises to ourselves erodes our integrity in the same way that breaking promises to others does. But more to the point here, when we mix up our important goals with low-value to-do items, we lose sight of what is and isn't a worthy priority. Before long, our days become a series of Pyrrhic victories over chores and er-rands as we lose more and more ground on those goals that matter most. We win our trivial to-do battles and lose the war to *significantly* change our lives. So please remember, a goal plan is more than a To-do list.

3. In Great Goal Plans Form Serves Function

Choosing what life goals to focus on can sometimes be daunting, messy, and a bit intimidating. But once you get clear on your priorities, your plan should become intuitive and easy to use.

The more parts in a machine, the more things that can break. Similarly, the more complex your goal planning sys-tem, the more rigid it becomes and the more that can go wrong with it. Overly complex systems can also trick you into thinking that over-planning somehow makes up for under-executing.

It doesn't.

The plan is always only a means to an end. **That end is achieving your goals and creating a life worthy of your potential.** What I call a *breakthrough* life.

Too many bells and whistles can be distracting, too. I sometimes check out goal planner or journaling videos online and have noticed that a lot of folks have planners that look like a bunch of Care Bears upchucked rainbows all over them. Every last item is highlighted with a differ-ent color, drawings, graphs, charts, and stickers galore.

I love highlighters, drawing, and stickers as much as the next Care Bear, but that's called "scrapbooking," or "art journaling," not "goal planning." One wonders where they find time to achieve any goals after putting so much time into prettifying their goal planners.

By contrast, billionaire Brit Richard Branson keeps a long list of goals on a piece of paper, in no particular order, with no deadlines. It doesn't get simpler than that.

While that's probably too simple to be effective for most of us, it does go to show that the magic of goal setting isn't in bells and whistles. The magic happens when form serves function, and we start actually *achieving* the goals we set.

4. Great Goal Plans Are Flexible

This one is closely related to form serving function. You and your goal plan must be adaptable to the changing realities and shifting priorities of your life. To mix metaphors: Don't marry your map. Reaching your destination is what matters most and the map is just a tool to help you get there. Sometimes the map will be wrong, and that's okay. When this happens, you simply take new bearings, correct the map, and change direction. You leave your map standing at the altar, and if need be, you mix your metaphors.

In other words, you stay flexible.

5. Great Goal Plans Focus On The Near-Term

Some success teachers advise creating a five-year goal plan. The idea is to imagine where you want to be in life five years hence and then work backward, listing all the goals and sub-goals required to get from here to there.

While this makes for a great motivating exercise (and we will be doing something similar later), I'm now convinced that it makes for a terrible goal plan.

Why?

Because the further out in time you project your plan, the greater the unpredictability, and therefore the less reliable your plan becomes. It's like the Heisenberg Uncertainty Principle of goal setting.

That isn't to say you should ignore your long-term goals, by the way. Only that your focus should be on near-term goals for this month, week, and year.

USING BREAKTHROUGH GOALS!

This book will help you check all of those boxes for creating a great goal plan. It's divided into four parts and a resources section.

Part 1: *The Anatomy Of Goals.* To achieve your goals, you must first be clear about what makes for a good goal and what doesn't. So we'll start there by defining *SMART* goals. (If you've heard of *SMART* goals before, don't skip this because the definition I use differs from most.)

Next, you'll discover the eight essential life domains where I believe you must have goals if you want to realize your full potential and live a breakthrough life.

Part 2: *Finding Clarity.* Here you'll do some mental and emotional slate cleaning along with some strategic prep work for creating your goal plan. After that, you'll create a powerful and exciting vision of your ideal future. You'll also have the option to choose an all-important aspiration called your *Definite Chief Aim.*

Part 3: *Crafting Your Plan.* Here is where you'll get into the nitty gritty of creating your goal plan. It may be challenging and a tad confusing at first, but it gets easier as you go along. That's often the way it is with great goals, so it makes sense that that's the way it must be with a great plan. You can handle it.

Part 4: *Achieving Your Goals.* Once you have a goal plan, you need the tools to work that plan and achieve the goals you've set. That's what *Part 4* is all about.

THREE TIPS

Here are three tips for getting the most out of this book.

Tip 1: Don't Skip Ahead. If you're itching to skip to *Part 3* so that you can start planning right away, please don't. The first two parts of the book are there for a reason: They are the bedrock on which you will build your goal plan. Without that solid foundation, your goals may tumble down when buffeted by the inevitable storms of life.

Tip 2: Create Your Plan ASAP. For the love of the goal gods, please don't read through this book with the idea that you'll return later to create your plan. Despite our best intentions, we both know how that usually goes. We read a new personal development book and feel excited about all the possibilities, then have dinner and plan to plan tomorrow. When tomorrow arrives, that initial excitement has faded, and we move on to the next exciting personal development book.

Most of us have done it. God knows I've done it more times than I can count. Please don't do it this time. Refuse to postpone or procrastinate your freedom and your future any longer. Reclaim your power now by creating your goal plan ASAP.

Once you reach *Part 3*, go ahead and read through it once to get a feel for the process, but then **immediately** re-read it while working through each step.

We respect our intentions, our goals, and ultimately ourselves by *doing*. By taking action on those things we claim are important, and crowning our covenanting words with deeds. This is the essence of integrity, maturity, and success.

Tip 3: Get A Goal Journal. Get a notebook for completing exercises and recording your progress on goals. This is your goal journal, and it's both an invaluable tool and a living record of your personal growth.

A NOTE ON GOAL PLANNERS

While you can plan perfectly well in your goal journal, there are also some great goal planners now available, and this system can be adapted to any of them. You can find three of my favorites in *Resources* 2 at the end of this book. And as a thank you for buying this book, you'll also find a link there for downloading a free copy of the *Breakthrough Goals! Planner*. These are planning pages I designed specifically for use with this system.

* * *

Okay. I've finished writing the *Introduction* so I can check that off my goal list for today:

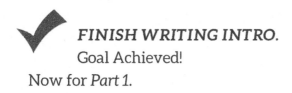

FINISH WRITING INTRO.
Goal Achieved!
Now for *Part 1.*

PART 1
The Anatomy Of Goals

Life isn't about finding yourself. Life is about creating yourself.
— GEORGE BERNARD SHAW

IF WE WANT TO LIVE GREAT LIVES, we need to have great goals. That's what *Part 1* is about.

First, we'll define *SMART* Goals, though in a way that may be slightly different from what you're used to if you've worked with *SMART* goals before.

Next, I'll show you a novel new approach for creating habit goals.

Finally, I'll describe the eight areas of your life in which you should have goals if you want to realize your full potential. I call these the *essential life domains*.

Now, without further ado, let's dive right in!

13

CHAPTER 1

SMART Goals

The time has come for man to set himself a goal. The time has come for man to plant the seed of his highest hope.

—NIETZSCHE

IN THIS BOOK, goals are very specific things defined by being very specific things. Which is to say, they aren't vague dreams or wishes like, "Get rich" or "Be A Writer," or "Be Healthier." Instead, goals are *SMART*.

You may have heard of *SMART* Goals before. There is more than one definition for *SMART* goals floating around out there, but this is how we'll define it: *Specific, Motivational, Actionable, Relevant*, and *Trackable*.

SPECIFIC means the goal is defined so that you know for sure if and when you've achieved it. "Get rich" isn't specific enough to be a viable goal. After all, what constitutes "rich," and how do you know when you've reached it?

On the other hand, "Have an income of $240,000 a year" is specific. You know precisely when you have achieved the goal and can put that lovely big red checkmark of victory in front of it.

As Jack Canfield says, "Vague goals produce vague results." If we want specific results, we need to set specific goals.

MOTIVATIONAL refers to your emotional and mental investment in the goal over the long haul. If you feel excited about a goal, that's fantastic, but motivation isn't just about how you feel. The more ambitious the goal, the longer it usually takes to achieve, and the more effort it usually requires. Success takes work. Early enthusiasm inevitably wanes, motivation invariably flags. Excitement was great fuel for launching us, but we need reasoned decision, sheer force of will, or both to keep flying.

We'll talk more about this in future chapters, but for now just remember to do a gut-check *and* a head check when deciding if a goal is motivating. Ask, "Do I want it?" But also ask, "Am I willing to *keep* wanting it even if I stop *feeling* like I want it?"

More questions to ask yourself:

- *Will I want this tomorrow or next week or next month when the newness fades?*
- *On a scale of one to ten, how much does this goal excite me?*
- *Am I willing to do what it takes to work on this goal, even when I don't feel like it?*
- *Am I willing to sacrifice time, money, and even other goals to achieve this goal?*

ACTIONABLE means the goal is something you yourself can take action on. As the hero of your own story, the action of pursuing and achieving your goals should center on you, and the way you define your goal should reflect this. The easiest way to tell if you have created an actionable goal or not is to look for a verb:

Write *500 Words On Goal Guide.*
Run *3 miles*
Complete *Duolingo German practice.*
Maintain *intermittent fast.*

Of course it takes more than just a verb to make a goal actionable. Consider, "Win the lottery." Despite the verb, this is a non-actionable (and silly) goal. Lady Luck alone determines whether you will succeed or fail there, and no action you can take will change that.

Even a worthy goal like "Get a $5/hr. raise" can be improved by clarifying the action. After all, you could be a great employee, ace every work review, force a smile through every asinine team meeting, and *still* not get that raise.

A much better goal would be, "Increase income by $800/month." Your *real* goal is to make more money, right? Well, getting a raise isn't the only way to do that. You could ask for a raise, *and* start a side hustle driving for Uber, *and* start a blog that you monetize with ads.

This isn't just about how you write your goals. It's about how you mentally, emotionally, and spiritually position yourself in the world: Will you be a passive spectator of your own life or an active creator of it? Making your goals actionable shifts your thinking from the passive to the active, from an external locus of control to an internal locus of control, from being an NPC to the hero of your own story.

RELEVANT refers to whether the goal genuinely reflects your desires and is in alignment with your values. While the other aspects of *SMART* goals are relatively cut and dry, relevancy is more subjective. It's about what your heart, gut, or conscience tells you.

You determine the relevance of a goal by asking questions like:

- *Is this goal right for me?*
- *Is this the right time for this goal?*
- *Am I feeling it?*
- *Am I mentally and emotionally ready for this goal?*
- *Is this really my goal, or am I doing it because I think I'm supposed to?*
- *Does this goal align with my values?*

Your questions may differ, and sometimes you'll need to ask few if any questions at all. If, for example, I've determined that writing and publishing this book is relevant to me, then I don't need to think about the relevance of every sub-goal, like finishing chapters one, two, three, and so on. The relevance of these steps is implied by the relevance of the larger goal they serve. In short, relevance is primarily about doing a gut-check for your most important goals.

TRACKABLE means the goal has a way for tracking your progress built right into it. You track a weight loss goal in pounds and a financial goal in dollars (or if you're a Brit, also pounds). My goal to write this book could be tracked in hours spent writing, word count, or finished pages.

Sometimes tracking is a simple binary of achieving or not achieving the goal: You meditated today, or you didn't. You dropped off the application, or you didn't. You asked her out on a date, or you didn't. You finished reading this sentence, or you . . .

WHAT ABOUT DEADLINES?

Most definitions of *SMART* goals define the "T" as "Time-bound," or something similar, and say you need to set a deadline for every goal. I reject this for three reasons.

First, deadlines are unforgiving and usually unrealistic. If you doubt me, write deadlines for every goal this year on your calendar, and come December 31st see how many—or rather how *few*—of those deadlines you met. Even if you achieved most of your goals, few of them will have been achieved "on time."

Second, even if you make a lot of progress on a goal, when you miss a deadline it makes you feel like you've failed.

Third, you simply don't *need* deadlines to achieve your goals when using the *Breakthrough Goals!* system.

I prefer to think in terms of **targets** because these are more realistic and forgiving than deadlines. Miss a target, and you simply take another shot. Cross a *dead*line, and what? A guy in a gun tower shoots you in the back? Even the word has some bad mojo.

19

The *Breakthrough Goals!* approach avoids that while keeping things simple: Since goals are set each month, week, and day at a time, your targets are always **implied**: "By end of day," "By this Sunday," "By the end of this month," or "By the end of the year." No deadlines required. No bad mojo.

Think of it like driving long distance in the dark. You don't need to see your destination to get there. Instead, you just need to focus on the road immediately ahead, illuminated by your headlights. And, mile by mile, you will progress until you reach your destination.

POORLY CRAFTED *VS. SMART* GOALS

On the next page take a look at some examples of poorly crafted goals versus *SMART* goals to get a clearer sense of how they differ.

I've included time targets in brackets for context, though you won't need to include these when setting your own goals, as I said.

Keep in mind that you don't always need to check every letter of the *SMART* box when setting a goal. It's just a helpful concept for evaluating your goals and optimizing them for success.

* * *

Now that we've gotten a handle on *SMART* goals, let's turn to one of the most important parts of goal setting and personal growth, *habits*.

POORLY CRAFTED GOALS	SMART GOALS
Lose Weight	**Lose 20 lbs. [by end of year]**
How much weight? By when? How will I know when I've succeeded?	*Nice and specific. I know when I've succeeded at this goal.*
Write Breakthrough Goals!	**Finish Draft 1 of BTGoals [this month]**
First draft? Final draft? The final printed version?	*Much better. I know precisely what needs to get done, and it's doable. I could also include a page number goal for tracking if I wanted.*
Get A Raise	**Request a $5/hr. raise [by end of week]**
How much of a raise? By when? How do I plan to go about "getting" it?	*This is precise and actionable. It shifts responsibility for outcomes away from my boss and onto me, where it belongs.*
Meditate More	**Meditate 20mins 5days/week [this month]**
How much more, Buddha?	*This is perfect, Buddha. It's specific, and it has a clear metric for tracking built in.*

CHAPTER 2

How To Turn Habits Into Goals

Success is the sum of small efforts, repeated day in and day out.
— ROBERT COLLIER

ABITS ARE NOTORIOUSLY DIFFICULT to turn into goals because they go on indefinitely, while goals always have one of two endpoints: *achieved* or *not achieved*. As a result, many people separate habits from their other goals and treat "daily habit tracking" as a separate exercise.

This is good.

But it's not great.

Few things beat the sense of accomplishment that comes from seeing an unbroken chain of red Xs or checkmarks stretching month after month across a calendar as proof of your commitment to maintaining a healthy habit. Habit tracking is good because this kind of long-view is powerful fuel for motivation.

But relying on habit tracking alone is not great because we are naturally teleological beings, which is just a fancy way of saying we need something to aim for—an end game to look forward to or a finish line to cross. We bookend our years with New Year's Days and New Year's Eves; our weeks with the weekends; and our workdays with clocking in, lunch breaks, and clocking out. It's how we think, how we work, and how we live our lives. And it's why we feel such satisfaction at putting a big red checkmark in front of a hard-won goal.

We get some of that with daily habit tracking, but we never quite get the big win we instinctively crave because the tracking never ends. It's like being first place in a race that has no finish line and goes on forever. After a while, you get bored of being a frontrunner in a race you can never actually win.

THE THREE RULES OF SETTING HABIT GOALS

To remedy this problem, I developed a method of converting habits into annual, monthly, or weekly habit goals using three simple rules: *The 240 Rule, The 20/30 Rule,* and *The 5/7 Rule.*

The 240 Rule

When choosing habit goals for the year, set a target to practice the habit or behavior two-hundred and forty out of three-hundred and sixty-five days in the year.

Example: *Meditate 240/365 Days.*

The 20/30 Rule

When choosing habit goals for the month, set a target to practice the habit or behavior twenty out of thirty days in the month.

Example: *Exercise 20/30 Days.*

The 5/7 Rule

When setting habit goals for the week, set a target to practice the habit or behavior five out of seven days in the week.

Example: *Morning Reading 5/7 Days.*

Now each of these habits has been converted into a *SMART* goal. You will still track your habits every day, but now they are directed at **distinct, timebound targets** each week, month, and year.

Why *The Three Rules*

You may be wondering why you shouldn't aim higher and set a goal to meditate every single day this year, exercise every single day this month, and read for half an hour every single day this week?

The short answer is that doing so is unrealistic and will only prime you for failure.

Imagine:

You have become a veritable Buddha, meditating every day for one hundred straight days. And then you have one of those days where everything that can go wrong does go wrong. Crisis management consumes the hours, and you are so exhausted by nightfall that you fall asleep before your head hits the pillow.

The next morning you wake up with a sinking feeling that you've forgotten something important—but you can't quite remember what it is. Then, as you rub the sleep from your eyes, it dawns on you: "I forgot to meditate yesterday!"

One hundred days of consistent meditation practice down the drain.

You blew it, Buddha.

Enlightenment is for winners, not slackers!

Can you see how ridiculous that would be? You have managed to redefine one hundred consecutive days of phenomenal success into total failure. This destroys whatever motivation you may have had to get back on the meditation horse, since now you have to "start all over."

The same applies to setting habit goals for every single day of the week or month. We imagine that if we set the bar at its maximum height, it will push us to excel more than we otherwise would. But usually, the exact opposite happens. We push ourselves too far, too fast, exhaust our motivation fuel too soon, and stop making progress. Or we just miss a day for whatever reason, because life happens.

The Three Rules—which you probably noticed are the same rule applied to different stretches of time—give you wiggle room for slipping up, taking a breath, or recovering after pushing yourself hard. In short, for being human.

If I do affirmations Monday, Tuesday, Wednesday, and Thursday but forget on Friday, it's no big deal because I still have two days left to hit my 5/7 target.

If a family crisis causes me to lose a week of writing this month, it's not the end of the world. I have ten days of wiggle room this month, so I can still reach my 20/30 goal.

And if I blew my meditation practice for an entire month, you won't see me panic. I'm Zen AF because I still have plenty of time left to achieve that 240/360 goal.

Om. Mofo.

Life rarely goes according to plan, so your plan needs to be flexible. *The Three Rules* are part of that flexibility.

Note that these rules don't *prevent* us from doing our habits every single day of the week, month, or year. I still can and do shoot for seven days a week on my daily disciplines. *The Three Rules* just give us a **realistic yet challenging success threshold**. Any success beyond this point is like earning an A+ instead of an A. Or, if you prefer, like icing on the goal cake.

Mmmmm. Goal cake.

OPTIONAL RULES

Here are two more optional rules that you may find helpful when planning and executing habit goals:

The Little Less Is More Rule

You might also call this the *Low Bar Rule*. Like I said, the purpose of *The Three Rules* is to set a realistic yet challenging success threshold for the number of days you work your habit goal. And while you shouldn't set a goal *above* that line, it's perfectly fine to set a goal *below* it. In fact, this is often the best thing to do when starting a new and challenging habit.

For example, instead of setting a goal to "Walk 2 miles a day 5 days a week," you start with a little less in terms of *frequency*: "Walk 2 miles/2 days a week."

Or a little less in terms of *distance*: "Walk 1 mile/5 days a week."

Or both: "Walk 1 mile/ 2 days a week."

The key takeaway here is: **Establish first, expand second**. In other words, when first setting out to instill a new habit, frequency matters most. The habit needs to become just that, a *habit*. Only after you've made it a habit should you try to expand it in terms of duration, length, intensity, and so on.

Weather permitting, I religiously walk at least two miles every day. But when I first began my walking discipline, my low bar goal was just to round a single block each day.

Once I got moving, I found it easy to go two or three or four blocks, especially since I knew that I'd already won that day after the first block and that anything beyond that was gravy.

Before long, my new low bar goal was to go three blocks, and walking a mile became the gravy goal. Later, a mile became the norm, so it became my new low bar. Two miles was now gravy.

Too high of a high bar can be daunting. But not goal gravy. Who doesn't want more goal gravy? It's almost as good as goal cake.

You'll find that when it comes to habit goals, starting with a low bar, working to establish the habit, and *only then* expanding it will lead to phenomenal (and compounding) results. When it comes to habit goals, a little less really is more.

The Make-up Rule

You may be wondering if you can have make-up days for missed habit goals. Using the previous example, if you failed to walk your one mile yesterday, can you walk two miles today and call it good?

I say, yes you can.

Mostly. Kinda.

It is always better to be consistent. After all, cramming a week's worth of habit goals into a single day defeats the goal of establishing a consistent habit.

On the other hand, you need to be adaptable, and it's better to walk that mile late than not walk at all.

So go ahead and make-up habits when you need to. But with one caveat: When tracking them in your journal or planner, make sure it's obvious that they are make-up habits. I use a purple pen instead of the usual red pen to distinguish tardy disciplines from timely ones, for example. Or, instead of marking it off with a big X, I might mark it off with a big M, for "Make-up."

Giving yourself room to make-up for missed habits while also identifying them as make-ups strikes a good balance between giving yourself wiggle room and being honest (and accurate) about your progress.

BREAKING BAD HABITS

You can set goals to break bad habits, too. The main difference is that using *The Three Rules* may not always be viable.

If you want to quit smoking, for example, you'd probably need to set a goal to stay smoke-free every day of the week, month, and year, 7/7, 30/30, and 365/365.

With that said, I recommend that you set bad habit abstinence goals for every single day *only* if it's essential for success in breaking the bad habit. Going on a social media fast for a month doesn't require the same commitment to abstinence as quitting vaping, for example. To break the social media habit, I might set a goal: "Go 20/30 days sans Facebook." Whereas to quit vaping I'd probably set a goal like, "Go 30/30 days vape free."

Replace The Reward

Typically, it's more challenging to break a bad habit than instill a good habit for the obvious reason that the bad habit is *already* a habit! And however bad the bad habit may be, it rewards us in some way, or we wouldn't continue engaging in it. So, when breaking a bad habit, it's best to simultaneously replace it with a better habit—one that's also rewarding.

Don't just stop your daily habit of pigging out on (glorious, delicious, and all-holy) cheesecake, for example. Replace it with a healthy and rewarding alternative, like an orange or a walk around the block.

Let's not kid ourselves, though: Some bad habits are so rewarding that no replacement will ever feel quite as satisfying, at least initially. It's a scientific and presumably Biblical fact that however good oranges and leisurely strolls may be, they aren't as good as cheesecake. The point of the positive replacement habit is to dull the edge of psychological "withdrawal" from the bad habit, while laying the groundwork for growing the new and better habit.

Which brings up another point: **Don't try to replace a hard-to-break bad habit with a hard-to-instill good habit.**

Most of us have made this mistake with diet and exercise, particularly. We're overweight, and the most activity we've seen in two years is a daily walk to the fridge (for cheesecake, of course). So we decide to go on a diet to break our unhealthy eating habits and replace them with healthy eating habits.

So far, so good.

But then we also decide that we're going to replace our nightly couch potato habit with working out an hour a day, five days a week, at *24 Hour Fitness*.

So far, so dumb.

Why? Because we will probably hate the workout routine. We're just not ready for it. We're already feeling angst and the cheesecakes withdrawal shakes . . . "And now I have to use this $#&@!!! Step machine for twenty minutes again? What was I thinking? And who invented this infernal torture machine anyway? Satan?"

The point of a positive replacement habit is to *reduce* **the pain of breaking a bad habit, not increase it.** So if it's a hard habit to break, choose a relatively easy positive replacement. The daily workout goal can wait. For now, just take that leisurely walk around the block.

Beating Addictions

For especially nasty habits, including those that rise to the level of dependency and addiction, I highly recommend reading *Beat Your Addiction: A Complete Program For Overcoming Any Addiction* by doctors Kenneth Peiser and Martin Sandry. Don't let the ugly cover design fool you. It's a fantastic resource that will teach you how to use Rational Emotive Behavioral Therapy to overcome addictions and addictive behaviors, including emotional addictions like negativity and anger.

Of course, consult with your doctor or mental health provider too, and all that other typical disclaimer jazz. But you know that already.

* * *

There you have it. *The Three Rules* (and two optional rules) of setting positive habit goals and tips for breaking bad habits.

Next, let's look at the eight domains of your life where you need goals if you want to thrive. But first, a couple of exercises.

Exercise: Identifying Bad And Good Habits

Step 1. In your goal journal, list any bad habits you want to break now or at some point in the future. Make another list of any good habits you'd like to develop now or in the future.

Step 2. Put a star next to the one bad habit you'd like to break first, if you had to choose. Put another star next to the one good habit you'd most like to develop.

Step 3. Refer back to this list when it's time to flesh out your goal plan.

Exercise: Addressing Addiction

If you have an addictive behavior that needs tackled, you probably already have that in mind as a goal. Now is a good time to do some preliminary research on counseling services, buy that Nicorette, find out where the nearest AA meeting is, or head to Amazon and order *Beat Your Addiction: A Complete Program To Beat Any Addiction*.

CHAPTER 3

The 8 Essential Life Domains

What you get by achieving your goals is not as important as what you become by achieving your goals.

— HENRY DAVID THOREAU

WHEN CREATING YOUR GOAL PLAN, you will set goals across different life areas that I call domains. If you want to achieve your full potential and live a breakthrough life, it's important to set goals in every domain. There are eight of them:

- *Health & Fitness*
- *Vocation*
- *Wealth*
- *Personal Development*
- *Relationships*
- *Spirituality*
- *Creativity*
- *Fun & Stuff*

Let's take a closer look at each. While reading the descriptions, have your goal journal handy to jot down any ideas and inspirations for goals that come to you. These will give you a head start once it's time to create your plan.

HEALTH & FITNESS

Alternate Labels: *Health and Wellness, Health/Wholeness, Physical, Body, Diet & Exercise.*

You probably don't need to be told to have goals related to your *Health & Fitness.* Americans spend upwards of sixty billion dollars each year trying to lose weight or get in shape, and the same three things top our New Year's Resolution lists every year: *Diet* or *Eat better, Lose weight,* and *Exercise more.*

In a sense, every other life domain depends on the goals you have in your *Health & Fitness* domain. After all, if you are chronically ill or woefully out of shape, you'll have a hard time achieving, let alone enjoying, your successes in other areas of life.

Even if you are already healthy and fit, you still need to have goals for maintaining that. In short, having goals in your *Health & Fitness* domain is non-negotiable.

Example *Health & Fitness* Goals:
- Research healthy diets.
- Exercise 3 days/week throughout February.
- Weigh ≤ 150 lbs.
- Take a 30 day drink break.
- Track food every day for thirty consecutive days.
- Join a yoga class.

- Do 100+ pushups without stopping.

WEALTH

Alternate Labels: *Money, Financial Freedom, Riches, Prosperity, Abundance.*

I used to call this the financial domain, but "financial" sounds grey and dull, like an insurance adjustor from 1954. "Wealth" sounds rich and green, like a forest full of money trees. Whatever you call it, this is about your bank accounts and bottom lines.

More fundamentally, it's about **freedom**.

Looked at a certain way, isn't that what money is? Freedom distilled into magical little pieces of paper that can transform into just about anything you desire: Books, clothes, cottages, cars, checks to charities, mansions, Mediterranean vacations, financial empires, flowers for mom, triple 20oz iced mochas, and most importantly, time.

Tony Robbins defined success as "doing what you want to do, where you want, with whom you want, whenever you want." The question that naturally follows this is at the heart of so many of our goals: "But how?" What is it that ultimately frees us to do what we want, when we want, with whomever we want, whenever we want?

Usually, money does it. *Wealth* does it.

Many—maybe most—of us have some seriously conflicted views about money that sabotage our *Wealth* goals. If that's you, set a goal to improve your relationship with money by learning about it. In *Resources 2* I share some books that helped me radically and positively change my mindset towards money and wealth creation (Which is saying a *lot*, since I was a crazy Communist for over twenty-five years!) Check them out.

Example Wealth Goals:
- Pay off credit cards.
- Create a budget.
- Read *Total Money Makeover* by Dave Ramsey.
- Build an emergency fund of $1000.
- Earn $7000 in a single month.
- Open an Acorns Investment Account.
- Research and identify top 5 side gigs.

VOCATION

Alternate Labels: *Career, Calling, Business, Entrepreneurship, Work, [Your Business Name Here].*

Vocation may or may not be the same as your day job. If you feel that your day job is your calling, or at least a career you plan to be in a while, great. Goals for that go here.

But say you are working as a barista just to pay the bills, while your true work happens every night when you come home and slap paint to canvass, slowly mastering composition and color with the goal of one day becoming a fulltime artist.

To the rest of the world, your efforts in painting may look like a hobby or avocation because it doesn't pay the bills.

But you know better.

You know that the day is coming when you'll grow prosperous as an artist. You know that art is your true calling.

So, your *Vocation* goals are all related to that, rather than pulling a better espresso.

On the other hand, say you have a vision of owning a coffee shop one day, but you also like making art. In that case, goals related to being a better barista may indeed be vocational because you want to know everything you can about the business, from the bottom up. It may be that—during this season of your life, at least—your art goals fit better under the *Creativity* domain.

Only you can decide what counts as a *Vocation* goal. Just don't think that it must be tied to income. It doesn't.

If You Are A Student Or Undecided

If you are a student, you may want to replace this entire domain with *School* or *Education*.

And what if you're stuck in a dead-end job you hate, have no "career," no sense of "vocation," or otherwise don't know what your "calling"' is?

Simple.

Make finding your calling a goal!

Then set out to achieve that goal (Chapter twenty-six, *Not Sure? Prototype* will show you how).

Example Vocation Goals:
- Incorporate my business.
- Reach 1000 followers on *Instagram*.
- Read 4 books on marketing.
- Set up my blog.
- Apply for [Dream Job Name] at [Company X].
- Work on Home Biz Project 2 hours/day, 5 days/week in March.
- Crush insignificant rebellion.

PERSONAL DEVELOPMENT

Alternate Labels: *Personal Growth, Self-Improvement, Learning, Study, Mind.*

This domain is a home for goals related to self-improvement and learning, including learning how to do more and be more.

The fact is, no one who wants to create a breakthrough life can be long content to know only what they already know, do only what they are already doing, or be only what they already are. Growth is essential.

The average CEO reads 60 books a year. And every goal guru worth his success salt emphasizes the importance of constantly increasing your knowledge, expanding your mind, and developing your skills.

In short, **there is no homeostasis in success.**

As Norman Mailer said, "Every moment of one's existence, one is growing into more or retreating into less."

Lou Holz put it more bluntly. "In this world you're either growing or you're dying, so get in motion and grow."

This is as good a time as any to point out that sometimes a goal can be equally at home in more than one domain. A goal to study the craft of writing, for example, could be a *Personal Development* goal, a *Creative* goal, or a *Vocation* goal. Go with what makes the most sense to you and for your life right now.

Example Personal Development Goals:
- Do affirmations 5 days/week for one month.
- Join/Create a Mastermind group.

- Make a vision board.
- Complete *Duolingo* German.
- Read 5 books about ancient aliens/history's mysteries.
- Take a life drawing class.
- Develop a morning wake up ritual/routine.

RELATIONSHIPS

Alternate Labels: *Family & Friends, Social, Interpersonal, Love.*

Goals in the *Relationships* domain are about honoring and nurturing meaningful relationships in your life. This includes romantic partners, your spouse, your children, your extended family, your friends, and even your pets.

It is here that you prioritize those you love by celebrating birthdays, renewing connections, going out on date nights, having adventures with friends, and calling mom. If you are single, here's where you might set goals related to finding that special someone.

Relationship Types

Some goal planning systems break this into multiple domains based on the type of relationship, such as having one domain labeled *Family* and another, *Friends.* Or one for *Romance/Marriage* and another for *Family/Friends.*

I think this approach is unnecessarily complicated and not a little irritating since—at least when there's a *Marriage/Romance* domain—the implication seems to be that single people are somehow incomplete. As a stubborn bachelor who is quite content in his stubborn bachelor-hood, I reject that notion. But if you want to divide this domain based on relationship types, that's fine too. As always, adapt my method to work for you.

Example Relationships Goals:
- Research dating profile creation best practices.
- Have four date nights this month.
- Pre-write birthday cards for all family and friends.
- Buy mom flowers, just because.
- Schedule coffee date with John and Sarah.
- Give three random compliments this week.
- Buy Spot a new chew toy.

SPIRITUALTY

Alternate Labels: *Faith, Soul Stuff, Spirit, God, Church, Synagogue, Devotion.*

I used to treat this domain as optional. Not anymore. I've seen too consistent a correlation between being stuck in life and neglecting the Spirit to ignore or downplay the importance of making time for the spiritual side of life.

I'm not saying that you have to belong to a specific faith tradition or even believe in God in any traditional sense. What I do mean is that nourishing your Spirit is key to achieving your most ambitious goals.

Dag Hammarskjold said, "The longest journey is the journey inward." It lasts a lifetime, possibly longer. Our Spiritual goals acknowledge that this *inner*life journey matters at least as much as the *outer*life journey.

Spiritual goals sustain us by infusing our every step with the strength to navigate challenging days, to keep the faith on self-doubting days, and to joyously, gratefully delight on those trouble-free days we might otherwise take for granted.

Determine what spirituality means to you and set some goals around that. Ask your deepest heart what it longs for. Make a habit of reading the sacred texts of your spiritual tradition (and those of other traditions, too). Attend religious services, practice deepening your prayer life, or start a meditation practice. If your soul sings when making art, or writing poems, or dancing, then look there for clues for evolving a personal spiritual practice.

However you do it, just don't neglect your Spirit. Or you'll be neglecting your truest and highest Self.

Example Spirituality Goals:
- Meditate 5 days/week in April.
- Go on a spiritual retreat.
- Read *The Bhagavad Gita*.
- Find my faith community (try out at least 3).
- Start & maintain morning prayer practice (20/30 days).
- Attend Mass weekly for three months.
- Stop being such a wicked sinner. (Joking!)

CREATIVITY

Alternate Labels: *Art, Poetry, Writing, Arts and Crafts, Muse Time, [Your Favorite Creative Outlet Here].*

I am convinced that creative self-expression isn't just for artists, musicians, and poets. Creativity is our very nature. In *Big Magic: Creative Living Beyond Fear*, Elizabeth Gilbert has a line that has some big magic of its own: "The universe buries strange jewels deep within us all, and then stands back to see if we can find them."

Creativity is treasure hunting. We dig using whatever picks and shovels we like: Guitars, garden tools, pencils, paintbrushes, pots and pans, blocks of wood, balls of yarn, yodeling, doodling, dabbling.

Creative self-expression is also one of the greatest secrets to success across all life domains because it expands your range of vision—**It teaches you to see the world in novel ways.** This ability to look at things and experiences with a creative eye leads to inspiration, innovation, and seeing opportunities where others only see obstacles.

Even if you don't think of yourself as particularly creative or artistic, I strongly encourage you to have goals related to creative self-expression. Your life will only become richer for doing so.

Example Creativity Goals:
- Write 500 words a day, 5 days/week in July.
- Pen five poems.
- Take an acrylic painting course.
- Set up my dream woodworking shop in garage.
- Cook an amazing seven course meal.
- Read/complete *The Artist's* Way by Julia Cameron.
- Build and launch my art blog.

FUN & STUFF

Alternate Labels: *Fun Bucket, Things-n-Stuff, Miscellaneous, Everything Else, Grab Bag, Just for Fun.*

This domain is for goals related to adventures, hobbies, things you want to own, or anything else that doesn't fall under the other domains.

Example Fun & Stuff Goals:
- Join a D&D group.
- Visit the museum.
- Buy a flux capacitor.
- Plant a garden.
- Travel to Mexico.
- Go back to the future.
- Learn to play the ukulele.

As you've learned already, it's best to create specific goals like "Learn to play three songs on the ukulele" rather than "learn to play the ukulele." But it's okay to break that rule in the *Fun & Stuff* domain. Here is where I like to indulge the little rapscallion within. He's sometimes naughty and doesn't like all my silly rules!

The older you are, the more important having goals in the *Fun & Stuff* domain becomes, too. Age naturally inclines us to seek greater and greater stability and security, which is smart. But as we age, we also need to be more deliberate about making time to do what once came naturally, play. If we don't, then we risk ossifying in body, mind, and spirit. So set some fun goals, you old coot. Just nothing too crazy. We don't want you to throw out a hip.

People, Places, Things

Suppose you're introverted or only have a few interpersonal goals focused on core relationships? In that case, you could merge the *Fun & Stuff* and *Relationships* domains to create a *People, Places, and Things* domain (*PPT* for short).

As a happily single homebody, I often do this. My *Relationship* domain usually has the same few goals each week, like calling my mom and meeting up with a couple friends. And since most of what I love doing falls under the *Vocation*, *Personal Development*, and *Creative* domains, my fun list was usually sparse, too. So, merging *Fun & Stuff* with *Relationships* to create a *PPT* domain has served me well. If you think it will serve you well too, then by all means adopt this approach.

FINAL TIDBITS

Let's conclude this chapter with some final domain related tidbits, and a couple of exercises.

Labels Are Secondary

As with the *PPT* example, don't be afraid to change-up, merge, or modify domains if doing so makes sense to you. **Having goals in each domain is what matters most, not how you label or organize them.**

Just make sure not to neglect any parts of your life described by those domains. If, for example, you want to combine *Vocation* and *Wealth* into a single domain, that's fine so long as you include vocational *and* financial goals.

Optional Domains

You may want to add one or two special domains unique to you, your life, and your goals. Anything that you feel should be a distinct life domain, is a viable life domain.

You are the boss of you.

Subdomains

If the number of goals in a domain gets unwieldy, it may be helpful to divide it into subdomains.

You might, for example, create a subdomain for *Family* and another for *Friends* under the *Relationships* domain, like some goal planners do. Or *Writing* and *Art* subdomains under *Creativity*, as I have been known to do.

Project And Temporary Domains

You may sometimes have a project that you feel deserves a domain of its own, whether or not it could also fit under a regular domain. This is especially useful if the project will take a month or more and has numerous sub-goals or steps.

For example, I recently spent a couple of months working on a small side gig selling tee shirts online. I didn't think it fit under *Vocation* because it was just an experimental project. And while it could probably have fit under *Wealth*—since the main point was to create a new revenue stream—I decided against that too, since it wasn't only about money.

My solution was to create a temporary *Tee Biz Project* domain. After two months, when my tee biz experiment was over, the domain dropped from my goal plan.

Color Coding Domains

While not mandatory, you may want to assign a color to each of your domains, either with highlighters or colored pens. This will help you think of each domain as its own special category of goals. It also makes daily planning more creative and fun.

Exercise: Decide On Your Domains

Take some time now to determine how you want to define your domains. If you think the eight-domain model described here will work for you, perfect! You don't need to change anything. But if your lifestyle would be better served by replacing the *Relationships* and *Fun & Stuff* domains with a *PPT* domain, decide so now.

Similarly, do you have a huge goal that will benefit from having its own temporary project domain? Or, are there any optional or subdomains you want to use? Now is the time to decide on these, too.

Finally, assign a color to each domain if you like, and make a color key in your goal journal.

Exercise: Brainstorm Some Goals

While we're not in the actual goal planning stage yet, go ahead and brainstorm some possible goals for each domain in your goal journal now.

Part 1 Takeaways

Successful and unsuccessful people do not vary greatly in their abilities. They vary in their desire to reach their potential.

— JOHN MAXWELL

1. The best goals are SMART

Specific, Motivational, Actionable, Relevant, and *Trackable.*

2. Remember *The Three Rules*

Use them to create habit goals.

- ✓ **The 240 Rule** tells you to set a habit goal for 240 out of 365 days each year.
- ✓ **The *20/30 Rule*** says you should only set a habit goal for 20 days out of the month.
- ✓ **The 5/7 Rule** says you should only set a habit goal for 5 out of 7 days each week.

3. The *Little Less Is More* Rule

It says you can set habit goals that are a little less than what you think you can do and slowly increase from there.

4. The Make-Up Rule

It says that it's okay to make-up for missed habit goals. Just don't make making up habits a habit!

5. The 8 Essential Life Domains

- *Health & Fitness*
- *Vocation*
- *Wealth*
- *Personal Development*
- *Relationships*
- *Spirituality*
- *Creativity*
- *Fun & Stuff*

Change them, merge them, or add to them—but don't neglect any domain when creating your goal plan.

PART 2
Finding Clarity

When people will not weed their own minds, they are apt to be over-run by nettles.

— HORACE WALPOLE

WE LIVE IN AN ERA of fabulous and historically unprecedented abundance and opportunity. So, if you're not already living the life you want, then something or a few somethings must be holding you back. It could be baggage from the past, pessimism about the future, low self-confidence, or some combination of these. In *Part 2*, we're going to get some clarity and break through your blocks.

First, you'll release drags from the past and do some other preliminary work for moving forward into a life of success. **This will prepare you**

Next, you'll prove to yourself that you are victorious by nature. **This will empower you.**

Finally, you'll create an inspiring vision of your ideal future. **This will inspire you.**

CHAPTER 4

Prepare

Be prepared.

— BOY SCOUT MOTTO

T HE DRIVE TO SUCCESS TOWN is rarely a smooth one. If we're lucky we have some nice long cruise controlled stretches with clear roads, blue skies, and scenic views. But at some point, inevitably, we encounter roadblocks and have to take detours from our planned route. Delays *happen*.

And while you can't always anticipate when, where, or how they'll occur, you can and should try to be reasonably well-prepared for them. Many a great goal has been derailed for want of preparation. Let's make sure that doesn't happen to you.

How?

Four ways: By welcoming challenges, releasing the past, identifying potential obstacles, and by shoring up your defenses against a dread foe named Resistance.

WELCOME CHALLENGES

It may seem counterintuitive, but one of the best things you can do at the very outset of your goal achievement journey is to **welcome challenges to your success.**

Consider: When confronted with obstacles and setbacks to ambitious and goals, we usually become frustrated or discouraged. But when you stop to think about it, that's a strange reaction to have. Did we *really* believe that we can set a challenging goal and yet face no *challenges* in achieving it? It's right there in the name, warning us ahead of time: "Hey, I'm a Challenging Goal. Just a heads-up. This is gonna be *challenging.*"

Yet, despite this, we act surprised and get upset when the inevitable obstacle comes along and fulfills its job description by challenging us. It's really kind of funny, actually.

I suspect we can never fully overcome whatever wiring it is that makes us wacky in this way, but we can minimize the worst effects of it. We do that by reminding ourselves that challenges happen, challenges are **inevitable**. That— no matter how good our plan, and no matter how firm our resolve to succeed—challenges *will* come to try us.

Based on what I've learned from T.V. sitcoms, challenges are like a mother-in-law. You wish they'd never come to visit, but since that's never going to be the case, the best thing to do is make nice and welcome them.

RELEASE THE PAST

Create your future from your future, not your past.
— WERNER ERDHARD

You may be wondering what forgiveness has to do with achieving your goals.

A lot.

Consider . . .

Goals are about building and living into a future worthy of your potential. They are forward-looking exercises in willed optimism. The last thing you need when pursuing your goals is emotional dead weight from the past holding you back.

That's what resentment is, and what it does.

And it's why, for most of us, forgiveness is a vital preparatory step for goal achievement.

The bigger your goals, the more energy they demand. We must be selective and discriminating in where and how we invest that energy. And that includes emotional energy. **You can't at the same time live forward with optimism and live backward with resentment—These two emotional energies are mutually exclusive.** If you hope to succeed at your goals, then you must sacrifice one of them.

I think you know which one.

To put it another way, preparing for a journey means making choices about what we can, can't, will, or won't bring along. If I'm going for a hike, I'd be a fool to stuff my backpack with an iron, an Xbox, and a desk lamp, especially when doing so will leave no room for a first aid kit, an emergency radio, and a flashlight.

Similarly, being prepared to achieve your goals is as much about knowing what emotional and mental baggage **not** to bring along on your hike to success as it's about knowing what **to** bring along.

What Forgiveness Is & Isn't

Too often, we think of forgiveness as a moral imperative. We remember, for example, Jesus' admonition to forgive not only seven times, but seventy times seven times.

Then someone we care about stabs us in the back, and the hurt burns so deep that we think, "Well, I'm no saint, I'm no Jesus. I can't forgive. I won't forgive."

But forgiveness isn't necessarily just a moral standard to live up to (or fail to live up to). It's also a **rational choice that liberates us**.

Forgiveness is not about letting those who have hurt or misused you "off the hook," either. It's about letting yourself off the hook of futile resentment and needless pain. As Nelson Mandela said, "Resentment is like drinking poison and hoping it will kill your enemies." Forgiveness is making the highly rational choice of refusing to drink any more emotional poison.

So, start there.

Prepare yourself to move on your goals with power and grace by releasing any emotional baggage of resentment, anger, blame, or hate you are carrying—Towards individuals, groups, society, yourself, even God, if need be.

Besides easing your emotional burden, forgiveness makes room for more of everything positive and good to enter your life. Optimism and enthusiasm will increase, becoming fertile soil for your goals to flower and for success to blossom.

Exercise: Releasing Resentment

Step 1. In your goal journal, name anyone for whom you harbor resentment, anger, and even hatred.

Step 2. Describe why you feel resentment towards them, and acknowledge those negative feelings. This is especially important if you feel guilty about having negative feelings like hate, since this only adds another negative feeling to the weight of resentment you're already carrying. That's nothing but futile masochism. It accomplishes nothing, and you deserve better.

Be as brief or as detailed as you feel you need to be on this step.

Step 3. Write out the following, or something similar: "I forgive you, [name]. I release you, [name]. I now declare my freedom." Imagine saying it to them, if that helps.

Then imagine walking away.

Feel released.

Feel liberated.

Know that it is in your power to be at last free from them and your past.

Step 4. Like any other habit, habits of thought don't vanish overnight. So when feelings and thoughts of resentment shows up, interrupt these patterns by succinctly restating forgiveness: "I forgive, release, and move on."

Alternately, deeply inhale while saying or thinking, "Forgive." Exhale while saying or thinking, "Release."

Refuse to dwell on past resentments. Instead, interrupt and release them whenever they occur. In time, thoughts and feelings of resentment will dissipate.

Step 5. If you want to go further in self-empowerment through forgiveness, consider wishing your nemesis well. I'm no saint, nor do I particularly want to be one, so my approach is to temper my good wishes with a dose of humor by saying to myself, "I wish you well [name the person] . . . And myself even better!" [Insert devilish wink here.]

IDENTIFY POTENTIAL OBSTACLES

If you already have some big goals in mind for the coming year, now is a good time to think about potential challenges or obstacles you may encounter while pursuing them. This is the essence of preparedness.

Think of Napoleon Bonaparte surveying the field before battle. He notes that thick of brambles here, that steep incline there—features of the terrain that might require him to adapt his attack strategy.

Or here's a less history-nerdy example you may recognize. Have you ever started a diet in the Summer without planning for Halloween, Thanksgiving, and Christmas with the extra challenges they always pose to sticking with a diet?

I certainly have.

Fall and Winter are where diets go to die a sumptuous and fattening death.

By modifying our plan before the holidays, we can eliminate the obstacle before it becomes one.

For example, I might decide now that the holiday fests are treat days where I can eat whatever I want, so long as I refuse to have leftovers. Or I might make-up for the extra calories by deciding to exercise more during those months. Or I might decide that the most realistic goal for the holidays is just to hold the line against gaining weight and that losing weight can wait until January first.

Exercise: Anticipate Obstacles

Step 1. In your goal journal, write down two or three big goals that you want to achieve this year.

Step 2. List the main milestones or steps for achieving each goal. Try to think of any significant obstacles or challenges to reaching each milestone that could come up. Write them down.

Step 3. Brainstorm possible solutions or workarounds to each of those obstacles. Refer back to this when it's time to flesh out your goal plan.

Don't go overboard here. This isn't about trying to anticipate every conceivable obstacle you could encounter. It's about looking for likely and significant roadblocks so you can have a contingency plan, or even avoid them altogether by planning an alternative route to your goal.

Try to anticipate significant obstacles that trigger emotional self-sabotage, too. Ask yourself questions like these, then brainstorm possible solutions:

- Are there certain months when you struggle with lack of motivation, depression, or seasonal affective disorder?

- Are there certain times of the day when you consistently feel unmotivated?

- Do certain objects, events, locations, or people trigger apathy, laziness, irritation, or other feelings that make it more challenging to achieve goals?

- How long into a goal do you usually go before making excuses and procrastinating? (Look there for cues and hidden emotional blocks that you can plan for or try to avoid entirely.)

SHORE UP YOUR DEFENSES

The greatest obstacles to achieving our goals usually come from within ourselves. This is called Resistance, and we will talk more about it in *Part 4*. In the meantime, you'll benefit from reflecting on those times that you've gotten in your own way or have been your own worst enemy. This will help you shore up your defenses against self-sabotage in the future.

Be brutally honest with yourself. Admit any weaknesses and character flaws that have contributed to failure or made you give up on your goals in the past. Let's call it the *BS Self-Review*.

Exercise: BS Self-Review

In your goal journal, reflect on how you BS yourself or otherwise get in your own way. Then commit to nipping that BS in the bud from here on out. Here are some questions to get you started:

Do you tend to make excuses?
Refuse to make any more of them.

Do you default to blame-gaming when things don't go according to plan?
Take 100% personal responsibility for your outcomes from now on.

Do you get bored quickly or regularly fail to finish what you start?
Vow dogged determination from here on out, promising yourself to grab onto the goal and not let go.

Do you have low discomfort tolerance and tend to give up as soon as you start to feel mildly uncomfortable or just unmotivated?
Realize that feelings are not a valid justification—in themselves—for giving up on a goal and that success lies just on the other side of discomfort. Push on. (More on this later.)

Are there people in your life that trigger failure or that you allow to suck you into their drama and negativity? Or are you using others as an excuse for not taking personal responsibility for your own life outcomes?
Set some boundaries. Not just for them, but for yourself in relation to them. (More on this later, too.)

This is an open-ended exercise for self-reflection and increasing clarity. It isn't about making yourself feel bad.

It's about honesty.

It's about owning your outcomes.

It's about integrity.

And it's about committing to doing and being better going forward so that, this time around, you **will** achieve your goals. You **will** break through to the next level.

* * *

By working through this chapter, you've built a solid foundation for future success in your goals. You've released energetic and emotional dead weight from the past, planned ahead for potential future obstacles, and shored up your defenses again self-sabotage.

So, hat's off to you!

Next, let's continue this theme of self-review from another angle by shining a light on how wildly successful you already are. Whether you realize it (yet) or not.

CHAPTER 5

Create A Victory List

No matter how often defeated, you are born to victory.
— RALPH WALDO EMERSON

YOU ARE A WIZARD of accomplishment, a success samurai, a goal achieving dynamo. You may not feel that way now, but consider the fact that through the course of your life you've had many ambitions, overcome endless setbacks, and had countless victories.

Some goals you pursued begrudgingly, because you had to or felt you had to. Some goals you tackled enthusiastically, because you were *hungry* for it and refused to let anything stop you from succeeding. Both testify to your extraordinary capacity for success, and—to wax a bit Nietzschean—they are evidence of the power of your *Will* (and/or your *Will to Power*).

Ever sweated your way through an interview and landed the job?

Ever mustered the nerve to ask that hot guy or gal out, despite feeling weak in the knees and lacking confidence?

Have you earned a degree, or graduated high school, or even just aced a class you thought you'd fail?

Have you lost weight before? (Even if you've later gained it back. Still counts.)

Have you quit smoking? (Even if you've later lit back up. Still counts.)

Raised a kid?

Bought a house?

Mastered a challenging skill?

Mended a fractured relationship?

Won the trophy?

Cut yourself free?

Did the right thing?

Did the brave thing?

Got back up?

Started anew?

Have you kept reading this far? (Definitely counts.)

Our capacity to achieve is in our very DNA, and I suspect it goes deeper than that. If you doubt your innate goal achieving capacity, just take a gander at a baby learning to walk. He falls on his face, cries, gets back up, falls on his face, cries, and gets back up again. The wonderfully stubborn little tike just doesn't know when to quit, so he never does quit. He just keeps trying until, at last, walking and even running become second nature.

For that matter, consider the prototypical directionless slacker who everyone loves to hate. In his twenties, unemployed, living in his parent's basement, empty cans of energy drinks littering the floor.

What is he doing?

Playing video games, of course.

Maybe for twelve or sixteen hours a day.

Obsessed over exquisitely beating the next boss, maxing his skill slots, conquering his virtual world.

Yes, even *he* is, clearly, an accomplished goal achiever. He just needs to accomplish some more mature and life-enhancing goals. ("Starting with getting a damn job," I assume his dad would say.)

WHY CREATE A *VICTORY LIST*?

One way to reclaim our power and confidence—especially during trying times or periods of feeling stuck—is to create a *Victory List* where we record our successes, past, present, and future.

The *Victory List* reminds us that . . .

Every fear we stared down in the past **is evidence that we can face and beat our fears again.**

Every crippling defeat that failed to cripple us for good **is evidence of our resilience.**

Everything we accomplished that we thought we never could, **is evidence of our ability to be tenacious and bold.**

Every success, big and small, **is evidence that we are born to victory.**

A *Victory List* will show you that "failure" is the exception in your life, not the rule. It also helps you recognize how often apparent failures later became steppingstones to greater success.

You'll realize, too, that you are already an accomplished goal achiever with an indomitable Will, when you choose to exercise it. The rule of your existence is success after success after success. Failure is just punctuation.

Exercise: Create A *Victory List*

Here's how to create your *Victory List*:

Step 1. Set aside forty-five minutes to an hour, or thereabouts, where you won't be interrupted.

Step 2. Assign and label your goal journal with each of the following: *Childhood Victories, Teen Victories, Young Adult Victories,* and if you're a wizened elder, *Mature Victories.* Alternately you can divide your list into *Childhood, Teens, 20s, 30s,* etc.

Step 3. List every victory you can think of, big and small, starting with your earliest childhood memories and working your way up to the present.

It can be helpful to focus on one year at a time, asking yourself what notable victories you can remember at age nine, ten, eleven, and so on.

Don't neglect those young victories, either. Reciting a poem in front of your seventh grade class may not seem like a big deal now, but remember how huge and terrifying it was to you at the time. The moral of the message in this kind of memory is this: "If that sweet, scared, innocent kid could be brave—surely the adult me can be brave too. If the child me could be victorious in childhood goals, I can be victorious in adult goals."

Step 4. Add to this list whenever you have a new success or if you happen to remember a past victory.

* * *

Refer to your *Victory List* whenever you doubt your ability to achieve your goals. Use it as an antidote to limiting, defeatist, and negativity-skewed thinking. Add to it regularly. Make it a living testament to the fact that you are, by nature, a victorious being. Because that's precisely what you are.

CHAPTER 6

Envision Your Ideal Life

All successful men and women are big dreamers. They imagine what their future could be, ideal in every respect, and then they work every day toward their distant vision, that goal or purpose.

— BRIAN TRACY

IKE I SAID IN *CHAPTER 1*, some goal-setting methodologies ask you to think about where you want to be five or ten years from now and then to list every step required to get there.

It's an impractical approach.

Don't get me wrong; I wish it did work because it appeals both to my love of detailed goal planning and my childhood dream of one day growing up to be Nostradamus. Which is rather to the point of why this approach is so flawed.

I'm not Nostradamus.

Nor are you. Presumably.

We can't see into the far-distant future.

Of course, we can, and should, plan. And we can even be reasonably confident that the plan will work . . . up to a point. But the further out into the future we try to project our plan, the hazier and less reliable it gets. Anything past about one year, and there are too many unexpected variables for a detailed plan to remain viable.

That said, you should still have a clear long-term vision of what your life will look like in the more distant future— A target towards which your plan aims, that highlights the most significant goals you'd like to have achieved, and how you'd like your life to look. A vision that doesn't worry about being *SMART*, but instead is painted in bright colors with broad strokes to inspire you and help keep you motivated for the long haul.

THE POWER OF VISION

History time.

I live in Portland, Oregon, the Willamette Valley. In the 19th century, when this was still largely an untamed wilderness, fliers and pamphlets were created to hype up the region and inspire Easterners to undertake the arduous journey across the Oregon Trail and resettle.

These fliers and pamphlets painted a fabulous and fantastical picture of the Willamette Valley as a sunny land flowing with milk and honey. A place with more than enough acreage for everyone, where the soil was so rich that all you had to do was toss some seed, sit back, watch the crops grow, and rake in the money.

As you might expect, this was an exaggerated picture of what the settlers found once they arrived. Many people who arrived did indeed thrive, but it never came as easily (or as quickly) as those pamphlets promised. They didn't find a land flowing with milk and honey, but they carved one out of the forest, with the sweat of the brow.

So, what's the point of this, my little Oregon State history segue? Just this: These brave settlers endured the long and arduous trek West by holding to a grand and inspiring vision of what life would be like once they finally arrived in Oregon Country. It helped to fuel their motivation, especially when facing hardship along the way.

I imagine some family, hundreds of miles from nowhere, huddled in a wagon, rain pelting down on the canvass cover. Unspoken fears—justified or not—of Indian attacks haunting their thoughts. By flickering candlelight, they again unfold that little pamphlet about the Willamette Valley. Distracting themselves from hardship and fear, they talk and plan and dream of the new life they will soon be living. It restores their courage and renews their determination to push on to that land of promise.

No matter what.

Exercise: Create Your Inspiring Vision

Let's learn from those brave pioneers and create a bold and exciting vision of your future life, about five years hence. One that can sustain you. One that will inspire and motivate you. One that will keep you moving forward when the going gets rough and you're tempted to turn back. Here's how.

Imagine that it's about five years from now, and you are precisely where you want to be in life. You're living the dream, whatever that dream is for you. Now describe that life in your goal journal, with vivid detail.

Don't write in the future tense about things you *will* accomplish and what you *will* have. Instead, write in the past and present tenses about what you have *already* accomplished and what you *currently* have.

Try to feel excited and grateful during this exercise. Just like you would if all you are describing had already come to pass.

Here are some prompts to help you map your vision:

- Are you wealthy? How much money do you have in the bank? What's your annual or monthly income?
- What's your vocation? How many hours a week do you work?
- What do you do for fun?
- Where do you live? What's your home look like? How is it furnished?
- How do you spend your time most days?
- Who is with you? What are your relationships like?
- Where did you recently vacation? How often do you vacation?
- What's your health and fitness level like?
- What have you accomplished, and what are you now achieving?
- What new skills have you mastered?
- How deep and vibrant is your spiritual life?
- What habits have you instilled, and what routines do you follow?
- What negative habits or fears have you overcome?

For this exercise, don't think small. Dream big. Follow the advice of Les Brown, who said, "Shoot for the moon. Even if you miss, you'll land among the stars."

Walk through your ideal future, letting it inspire you with *possibility*. Engage your senses and feelings . . .

Seeing it.
Hearing it.
Smelling it.
Feeling it.

Infuse your subconscious mind with desire in the language it best understands: **emotionally evocative imagery**. Your subconscious will, in turn, get to work on ways to make your inspirited vision, or some version of it, a living reality (More on this in *Chapter 16, Change Your Mind*).

Revisit your vision often, making it familiar and real to your imagination. Turn to it whenever enthusiasm flags, self-doubt raises its ugly head, or you just need a reminder of why you set out on this goal achieving journey in the first place.

* * *

That's one damn fine inspiring vision you have there. Hat's off to you! Now, if you already have one colossal life-changing goal in mind as part of that vision, the next chapter is especially for you.

CHAPTER 7

Your Definite Chief Aim

There is one quality which one must possess to win, and that is definiteness of purpose, the knowledge of what one wants, and a burning desire to possess it.

— NAPOLEON HILL

POPULARIZED **BY NAPOLEON HILL** in *Think and Grow Rich*, a *Definite Chief Aim* is a single, huge, and hugely important goal that becomes your primary life focus, usually for many years. It's the goal that all your other goals either serve or are sacrificed for, if necessary.

Think of the athlete whose life revolves around training for the next Olympics. Or the gal who eats, sleeps, breathes, and saves for the down payment on her dream home. Or the guy who says, "Enough is enough!" radically changes his eating habits, and starts working out every day until he transforms from Dud to DILF.

If there was one word that best describes *Definite Chief Aim*, it is **obsession**.

It's *that* kind of goal.

If you don't (yet) have any goals that rise to the level of a *Definite Chief Aim*, don't fret. Having a *Definite Chief Aim* isn't required to complete your goal plan, since each year you'll have three life-shifting breakthrough goals that fill similar shoes.

Rest assured, a *Definite Chief Aim* will appear to you at some point. In the meantime, just pursue your breakthrough goals and follow your plan.

Don't try to force it.

Definite Chief Aims are like the A-Team. You don't find them, they find you.

If you do already have a monumental goal that keeps you awake at night, write it in your goal journal using the formula below.

HOW TO COMPOSE YOUR *DEFINITE CHIEF AIM*

This is the *Definite Chief Aim* formula as described by Napoleon Hill.

Step 1: Define what you want.

Be precise. If it's an amount of money, then write down the dollar amount. If you want to buy your dream home, describe its size, value, and key features. If you're going to be successful in any area, be specific about what that success looks like.

Step 2: Decide on what you will give in return.

This speaks to effort and integrity. What are you willing to give in time, spirit, talents, and dogged determination to realize your goal? Note that this doesn't have to be highly specific, like in *Step 1*.

Step 3: Decide on the target date.

I don't advocate setting deadlines for goals, but we'll make an exception for the *Definite Chief Aim*. Who am I to argue with the great Napoleon Hill?

Step 4: Create a plan of action.

Good news! The rest of this book is about creating your goal plan, so you're covered for *Step 4*.

Step 5: Write it down.

Based on what you decided in steps one to three, write out your *Definite Chief Aim*. Then sign and date it. This is a contract with yourself and the universe.

Step 6: Read it aloud twice a day

This is best done first thing in the morning and at night, immediately before going to bed.

EXAMPLE *DEFINITE CHIEF AIM*: BRUCE LEE

Let's end this chapter with a famous example of a *Definite Chief Aim* that you can use as a template for creating your own . . .

My Definite Chief Aim

I Bruce Lee will be the first highest paid Oriental super star in the United States. In return I will give the most exciting performance and render the best of quality in the capacity of an actor.

Starting 1970 I will achieve world fame and from then onward till the end of 1980 I will have in my possession $10,000,000.

I will live the way I please and achieve inner harmony and happiness.

— Bruce Lee Date: 1969

Part 2 Takeaways

It is your attitude, not your aptitude, that determines your altitude.
— ZIG ZIGLAR

Here are the key takeaways for *Part 2*:

1. Prepare

A little prep effort now will make your success journey smoother. Not *perfectly* smooth, but smoother!

- ✓ Welcome challenges. They are inevitable.
- ✓ Forgive and release the dead weight of resentment. Don't let pains from your past keep you one minute longer from living a successful and joyous life.
- ✓ Think about possible future obstacles to your most important goals so you can prepare for them or avoid them entirely.
- ✓ Do a *BS Self-Review* and start getting out of your own way.

2. Create a *Victory List*

Celebrate your accomplishments, big and small. Include childhood victories, too. These were significant at the time and are still worthwhile reminders of your innate capacity to meet challenges and be victorious.

3. Create a long-term vision

Imagine your ideal life five years from now. How do you want to look and feel? How much income do you want to have? Where do you want to live? What do you want to have accomplished? Paint an exciting picture of your best life and come back to it often as a source of inspiration and motivation.

4. Define a *Definite Chief Aim*

Focus on one major goal—your primary life focus for the next few years. If you don't yet have a *Definite Chief Aim*, that's okay. You'll find one naturally in time as you continue to set and achieve your goals.

PART 3
Crafting Your Plan

If you go to work on your goals, your goals will go to work on you.
If you go to work on your plan, your plan will go to work on you.
Whatever good things we build end up building us.

— JIM ROHN

T HE PROCESS OUTLINED in the following pages is not meant to be the final word on goal planning. Nor do I claim that it's entirely my own: I've curated, modified, and integrated the best of everything I've learned over many years of studying goal achievement.

I recommend that you follow the approach I outline here, just as I've written it. Feel free to modify the method later if you want to, but test it out a few times first. Even Picasso learned the rules of drawing and painting before he was ready to break and reinvent them.

When creating your goal plan, set aside a few hours where you won't be disturbed or distracted. Turn off your computer, phone, and television. Hang a "Do Not Disturb" sign on your door. Let your family members or roommates know that, unless there's a zombie apocalypse, they'd better not bother you or there'll be hell to pay. You got big, important, top-secret stuff going on and don't have time for their nonsense!

Tidy up your space the day before doing this if you need to. A chaotic environment leads to muddled thinking.

If you want to play some music while goal planning, that's fine. Just choose classical or relaxing instrumental, and no radio with DJs or commercials to interrupt your mental flow with their yippity-yapping.

You will build your breakthrough goal plan in five steps:

Step 1: Creating a *Dreamlist*.
Step 2: Creating your plan for the year.
Step 3: Creating your plan for the month.
Step 4: Planning your current week, and then each day.
Step 5: Doing regular *Progress Reviews*.

Now, for what you've been waiting for . . . let's build your goal plan!

CHAPTER 8

Create Your Dreamlist

If you limit your choices only to what seems possible or reasonable, you disconnect yourself from what you truly want and all that is left is compromise.

—ROBERT FRITZ

IF YOU ARE A COMIC BOOK NERD, think comics. If you are a movie nerd, think movies. In each case, the first panel or scene is often an "establishing shot"—A panoramic view of the whole city before the camera zooms progressively closer. From cityscape . . . then to a single street . . . then to a building . . . then into a room . . . then to the face of the protagonist.

This is how we're going to approach creating your goal plan. We start with a *Dreamlist* where you'll have a lifetime of goals and dreams in a single establishing shot. Like a bustling city, your *Dreamlist* is moving, vibrant, sometimes chaotic. It has everything from corner bistro sized goals to towering skyscraper dreams.

After creating your *Dreamlist* we'll zoom in on your year, then month, then week, and finally, day. But first, the establishing shot.

WHAT IS A *DREAMLIST*?

A *Dreamlist* has three main uses:

1. Backburnering goals. When you have goals that you want to achieve but can't prioritize right now in life, you put them on the backburner, your *Dreamlist*, to simmer until you're ready to focus on them.

2. Capturing ideas. Emerson said, "In every work of genius we recognize our own rejected thoughts; they come back to us with a certain alienated majesty." Most of us have had this experience with a book, movie, or invention: "I had that same idea years ago!" we exclaim. But we failed to act, so the idea moved on to more receptive minds.

The Muses are vain. If you don't bow in grateful homage when they deign to grace you with their presence, they will take their inspiration elsewhere.

Moral of the story: **Never leave an idea for a goal—big or small—in your head.** Use your *Dreamlist* to capture it, or it will likely soon vanish into the ether of forgetting.

If you later change your mind about that goal, simply strike it off the list.

3. Recording Dreams. *SMART* Goals are essential to success in life, but we must not neglect our more intuitive and imaginative side. The side that dreams of our fantastic future rather than plans for it. The *Dreamlist*, as the name makes clear, is the place to honor that part of yourself.

What constitutes a dream?

Any desire, vision, or ambition that inspires you, however unrealistic and Not-*SMART* it may be.

Sometimes, too, today's wild dream may mature into tomorrow's realistic goal. In 2021 "Travel To Mars" may be crazy talk. But in 2031 or 2041, hopping the SpaceX Express may be entirely doable (Thank you in advance, Elon Musk).

HOW TO CREATE YOUR *DREAMLIST*

Set aside thirty minutes to an hour where you won't be disturbed. Put on some relaxing or inspiring music if you like. Use your goal journal or loose sheets of paper. No computer. No phone. No typing. Pen or pencil to paper only.

Step 1: In your goal journal, assign dream pages for each life domain. Label them, *Health & Fitness Dreams, Vocation Dreams, Wealth Dreams*, and so on. I advise leaving two or three blank pages between each list so that your dreams will have room to grow over time.

Step 2: Brainstorm every goal or dream you can think of for each domain. Number them or use a bullet list, whichever you prefer. **Try not to stop until you have reached at least twenty dreams or goals for each domain**. This will be easy for some domains. For others, you may have to work at it a bit.

And that's all there is to it!

DREAMLIST TIPS AND POINTERS

Okay. That's *almost* all there is to it. Here are some tips and pointers for getting the most out of your *Dreamlist*.

Don't Be *SMART*

Don't worry about making your goals *SMART* here. Doing that can be detrimental during the *Dreamlist* stage because you want to maintain a flow of inspired and inspiring ideas and not get bogged down with details or format.

Don't Censor Your Dreams

Don't omit any goals or dreams from this list because you think they are childish, foolish, or unrealistic. When you honor these seemingly silly dreams by writing them down, you are respecting the source of your creativity, your subconscious mind. It will thank you with even more inspired insights and dreams while tirelessly working to make what you thought was impossible, possible.

Most great inventions and innovations were once scorned as "impossible" dreams, as I said earlier. Please remember that.

Remember too what Arthur Schopenhauer said of truth, because it applies to many a great Dreamer's dreams:

All truth passes through three stages. First, it is ridiculed. Second, it is violently opposed. Third, it is accepted as being self-evident.

Go With The Flow

While working on one domain, a goal idea for another domain may pop into your head. When that happens, turn to the appropriate domain dream page and write the goal down where it belongs. Then return to the domain you are currently working on.

We may not always be sure what domain a particular goal belongs with. "Is doing Yoga more about *Health & Fitness* or *Spirituality*?" If that happens, don't think too hard about it. Just go with what seems best right now. You can reassign the goal or dream to a different domain later if you want.

You Can Say That Again

It's okay to be redundant on your *Dreamlist* if doing so reflects how you think about your goals and dreams. Earn $100k/year, Earn $500k/year, Have $2,000,000, and Be fabulously rich are all legitimate items for your *Dreamlist* because you may think of each of these as steps along the path to a larger goal, or even as distinct goals.

This isn't the place to work out their relationship to each other. That comes later. Here it's all about capturing the goals or dreams that come to you, as they come to you.

Keep Adding To Your *Dreamlist*

Whenever a new dream or goal inspires you, add it to your *Dreamlist*. When your current goal journal is full, transfer your *Dreamlist* to a new goal journal.

It's entirely okay to let go of goals that you've outgrown, too. Never feel like pruning your *Dreamlist* of items that no longer speak to you reflects failure. Your *Dreamlist* should and will continue to change and evolve as you change and evolve.

* * *

Excellent. Now that you have your *Dreamlist* as an establishing shot for your future, it's time to zoom into your one-year plan. This is the most intensive part of the goal planning process, so have yourself a little stretch, grab yourself a cup of coffee, and meet back at the next page in fifteen.

CHAPTER 9

Plan Your Year

A year *from* now you may wish you had started today.

— KAREN LAMB

YOU HAVE AN INSPIRING LIST OF DREAMS, now it's time to tether some of those dreams to earth and create a plan with actionable goals, starting with those you want to accomplish this year.

Like I said earlier, we don't want to plan too far into the future. But we don't want to be too short-sighted when planning our goals, either. Focusing only on this week or month without giving a thought to where you want to be a year from now can lead to a lot of wasted time and energy. Admittedly, more productively wasted time and energy than it might be otherwise, but still wasted in terms of effective progress towards long-term change and success.

I have found that framing critical goals by the year strikes just the right balance between these two extremes of having too long-term a focus on the one hand and too short-term a focus on the other.

YEARLY PLANNING TIPS

Here are four tips for working through the yearly planning steps in this chapter.

Tip 1: Focus Only On This Year

The plan you're about to create is a "this year" plan and not a twelve-month plan. In other words, your plan begins now, with whatever month you are currently in, and continues through December 31st. Then, on January 1st of next year, you will start a new plan covering a full calendar year. (Alternately, you can plan from birthday to birthday.)

Tip 2: Do A Read-Through

I advise reading through all of *Part 3* to get a feel for this planning method. Then immediately come back and work through the steps.

Tip 3: Do A Rough Draft

Since identifying our priorities for the year can be messy, do a draft version first. Once you are clear on what you want to accomplish, you can create a nice, tidy, organized one-year plan using your goal journal, my free *Breakthrough Goals! Planner* (See *Resources 2*), or any other goal planner you choose.

What Ernest Hemingway famously said of novels applies to goal plans too: "First drafts are shit." And that's okay. It's just part of the process. So, allow yourself to be messy with your first draft.

Tip 4: Take Your Time

Please don't rush this part of your plan. This step is the longest, and it may be a bit confusing your first time through. But if you take your time and stick with it, I promise that your efforts will pay off later.

It's like when you let the dishes pile up. Washing, drying, and stacking them all can be time-consuming and messy. But once they are all clean and dried and put away, you can keep that from ever happening again by just doing your dishes as you dirty them.

Likewise, investing the time to bring order to the chaos of your ambitions here and now at the one-year level will pay off later by making your monthly, weekly, and daily planning a breeze.

HOW TO PLAN YOUR BREAKTHROUGH YEAR

Set aside some time when you will not be disturbed and put on some relaxing or inspiring music, if you like. Pull out your goal journal, planner, or some loose sheets of paper. Follow these steps:

Step 1: List Your Domains

Write down your domains. Under each, make a list numbered one through five.

Step 2: Transfer Incompletes

If there are any unfinished goals from last year's plan that you still want to achieve, transfer them to this year's list. You can skip this step your first time planning.

Step 3: Choose Some Dreams

Review your *Dreamlist* and circle **the top three to five goals or dreams in *each* domain** that you'd like to achieve or work on this year. That's three to five goals for *Health & Fitness*, three to five goals for *Vocation*, three to five goals for *Wealth*, and so on, **for a total of twenty-four to forty goals for the year**.

As you probably guessed, you'll be adding these to the five-goal lists you created in Step 1. But first . . .

Step 4: Define Milestone Goals (As Needed)

Create a section in your goal journal labeled ***Projects***. This is where big goals are divided into their component milestones and steps (The *Breakthrough Goals! Planner* includes a projects page).

Look at the dreams you chose in Step 3. Ask yourself if any are too big to be realistically achieved in one year. Now break these down into smaller, actionable goals—aka *milestones*—**that you *can* realistically achieve this year**.

Once you've done this, choose one more of these milestones as goals for the year.

For example, say your dream is to have an income of $10k a month. Since your current income is $2k a month, you decide this goal is too ambitious for a single year. So you break it into milestones on a *Project* page:

Goal: Reach $10k/month Income
Milestone 1: Reach $4k/month income.
Milestone 2: Reach $6k/month income.
Milestone 3: Reach $8k/month income.
Milestone 4: Reach $10k/month income.

Reviewing your list of milestones and thinking about how much you can accomplish this year, you decide that reaching the first milestone of $4k/month strikes just the right balance between ambitious and crazy. So you make it one of your top-five *Wealth* goals for the year.

After adding some other goals from your *Dreamlist*, your top-five list of *Wealth* goals for the year looks like this:

Wealth
1. Increase income to $4k/month.
2. Pay off Discover Card balance in full.
3. Pay off Capital One balance in full.
4. Pay off personal debts in full.
5. Save six-month emergency fund of $6k+.

Alternately, maybe you decide that reaching that second milestone of $6k/month is doable this year after all. In that case, you need to include it **and** the previous $4k milestone on your top five *Wealth* goals list. In other words, **don't leapfrog over milestones when setting one-year goals.**

Of course, now that you have two income milestones on your list, one of the other goals you were considering will have to go, since you only have room for five *Wealth* goals. So, you choose to axe "Pay off Capital One balance in full."

Now your list looks like this:

Wealth
1. Reach $4k/month income.
2. Reach $6k/month income.
3. Pay off Discover Card balance in full.
4. Pay off personal debts in full.
5. Save six-month emergency fund of $6k+.

In your career as a goal planning and achieving wizard, you'll frequently need to divide big goals into smaller milestones in this way. But I advise against doing this directly on your one-year goal list, or it may become a confusing mess. **Your one-year goal list is meant to summarize key objectives, not become a detailed outline of every milestone and sub-step required to achieve each goal. Use *Project* pages for that.**

Step 5: Shine And Polish

You should now have a draft list of your goals for the year, with three to five goals in each domain. That was the messiest part. Now, let's shine and polish each goal to create a bright, shiny, beautiful one-year plan.

Assign True Deadlines

Like I've said, as a rule we don't do deadlines in the *Breakthrough Goals!* system. But every rule has its exception, and the exception here is *true deadlines.*

What are true deadlines?

They are deadlines that you didn't set or can't change. Like fling taxes by April 15th, or the last day you can enter a short story contest.

If any of your goals have a true deadline, write it next to the goal on your one-year plan.

Make Each Goal *SMART*

Now is the time to make those dreams SMART.

- ✓ Make each goal **Specific**, so you know precisely when and how to accomplish it.
- ✓ Ask yourself if each goal is mentally and emotionally **Motivating** enough to hold your focus all year (or until it's achieved).
- ✓ Make sure that each goal **Actionable** and that success depends on your own efforts.
- ✓ Confirm that each goal is **Relevant** to who you are and want to be.
- ✓ Check that each goal is **Trackable** with a built-in way to measure your progress, like dollars, miles, pounds, hours, and so on.

Apply The 240 Rule

If you have any habit goals, formulate them according to the *240 Rule*. As in, "Exercise 240/360 days."

Step 6: Choose 3 Breakthrough Goals For The Year

Now that you have chosen all your goals for the year, across every domain, pick **three** that are the most important to you.

Highlight or circle them.

These are your breakthrough goals for the year. They are goals that, if achieved, would cause a quantum leap in the quality of your life, empower you to do more and be more than ever before, and bring you that much closer to the ideal life you visualized in *Part 2*. In short, **they are your most important and ambitious goals at this point in your life.**

Here are some more things to consider when choosing your breakthrough goals:

- Achieving even one of them would transform your life and make the year a huge win.

- Look to your emotional response: Breakthrough goals are often inspiring, a bit frightening, or both.

- Breakthrough goals are often ones that we have tried and repeatedly failed to achieve, year after year.

- The reason identifying breakthrough goals is so important is that you must be prepared to sacrifice for them. Time, energy, and the other goals on your list, if need be.

- Your breakthrough goals are your highest priority this year. **No other goals are allowed to compete with them.**

Step 7: Finalize Your Plan

When focused on our goal-trees, we may lose sight of the plan-forest, so take a couple of minutes to look over your plan with an eye to potential errors, conflicts, oversights, or opportunities for improvement.

- Make sure that you have at least three goals in each domain and no more than forty goals total for the year.

- Do a gut-check on your breakthrough goals: Are they *really* the most important goals for you this year?
- Look at your *Project* pages: Does everything look in order?
- Are you settled on those colors for each domain?
- Does anything else need to be changed?
- If everything looks in order, create a clean final written version of your one-year goal list.

You now have a massive list of inspiring and actionable goals for the coming year, including three seismic-sized breakthrough goals. This alone puts you miles ahead of most people, who never take the time to plan their future, beyond perhaps a handful of usually ineffectual New Year's resolutions. Congratulate yourself! You deserve it.

FINAL THOUGHTS AND TIPS

Here are some final thoughts and some tips on creating your one-year goal list.

Why Three To Five Goals?

You may wonder why you are limited to five goals in each domain. It's because, as Jim Rohn famously said, "You can have anything you want, you just can't have everything you want."

There are only so many hours in a day and days in the year to accomplish our goals. Yet, in the excitement of goal planning, we tend to overestimate how much we can achieve in a year. Too often, the result is a bar set so unrealistically high that our successes end up being overshadowed by our more numerous "failures."

That's not a recipe for motivation, sustained effort, and success. Mature goal achievers recognize the importance of prioritizing their goals, which sometimes means making difficult decisions about what to focus on and—just as importantly—what *not* to focus on, at any given time. I sometimes call this *The Rule Of Suck*, which says you have to be willing to suck at some things (at least for a while) if you want to excel at others.

Five goals in each domain may not seem like much for an entire year, but keep in mind that this adds up to forty goals total—Nearly a goal a week every week for a year. That's a tall order that few of us can reasonably hope to accomplish.

That too is good, by the way. Having more goals than we are likely to achieve in a year keeps us from growing complacent while at the same time forcing us to stretch and grow. The fact is, anyone who accomplishes all their goals in a year probably hasn't set sufficiently challenging goals.

On the other end, I recommend having **no less than three goals in a domain.** Even though we must prioritize some domains over others at different stages of our lives, we should never entirely neglect any domain.

It's great for Jack to focus on his vocation this year, but all work and no play makes Jack a dull boy. While all play and no work makes him a broke boy. And all personal development and no relationships makes him a lonely boy. Jack can give the lion's share of his focus to his vocation, but he needs at least a few goals in his other domains too.

And so do you. (Remember this when we get to planning your months and weeks, too).

In short, too many goals will set you up for feeling like a failure, while too few goals will limit your growth, potential for success, and quality of life. I've found that the Goldilocks Zone for a one-year goal plan is to have three to five goals in each domain.

Diversify Difficulty Levels

Consider including one or two relatively easy goals and one or two challenging goals in each domain.

This goes back to the Goldilocks Zone idea. Some easy wins throughout the year can fuel your momentum and lead you to accomplish more challenging goals. Plus, focusing day in and day out on demanding goals can be exhausting. Sometimes we just need a light day and an easy win.

At the same time, we need those challenging stretch goals because they do the heavy lifting of building our fantastic future and transforming us into our best selves.

Trading Off Between Domains

If you want to dominate in one domain more than the others this year, it is entirely okay to go beyond the five goal threshold. With one caveat: **Don't exceed forty total goals for the year.**

If, for example, you decide to have eight goals in the *Creative* domain, you must sacrifice three goals from somewhere else (while at the same time remembering not to drop any domain below the three goal minimum).

Let's simplify that with a rule: **No more than forty goals for the year, no less than three goals for any domain.**

Do A Lifestyle Check

This is similar to what we talked about in *Chapter 4.* Now that you have chosen your goals, think about your current lifestyle, how you spend your time, and how that might impact your ability to achieve your one-year goals.

You don't have to write all this down (though you can if you like). The point is to look for potential conflicts or problems that stand out, and to modify your plan accordingly. Here are some questions to explore:

- *How many hours a day and a week do I have to invest in my goals?*
- *Can I find more time for my goals? Where?*
- *Are there activities that I can or should cut out or cut back on so I can focus more on my important goals?*
- *Am I truly willing to sacrifice X to accomplish Y?*
- *What parts of my current lifestyle may get in the way of success or slow down my progress?*
- *Are there people who may be stumbling blocks? How could I deal with or prepare for that?*
- *Are there people who may support me in this goal? What help will I ask for?*
- *Are all these goals relevant to me right now in life?*
- *If I could only achieve one of my breakthrough goals this year, which would it be? (Consider putting an extra asterisk or a big "#1 Goal!" next to that one).*

When the Roman Catholic Church evaluates someone for sainthood, they assign a priest to be "The Devil's Advocate." His job is to give the strongest arguments for why the person should **not** be sainted. If the pro-saint crew can beat those arguments, then the person has proven worthy.

You might consider doing something similar, at least with your biggest, scariest, most exciting goals. Argue both the prose and cons, for and against your goals, to the best of your ability.

Even if you don't go that far, do challenge yourself here. It's okay to be uncertain and even intimidated by the goals you've set for yourself this year. But if despite that uncertainty you are still committed to trying, then that is a good sign that the goal is important and that you should go for it.

If You're Unsure Which Goals To Choose

If you're not sure what goals to prioritize for the year, you may be a tad bit too stuck in your head. Ask yourself what your *heart* has to say and give it room to answer. Here are some emotional clarity questions you can explore in your goal journal:

- *Where do I want my life to be next year? What goals on my list best serve that vision? What goals may run counter to it?*

- *Where do I want to be in five years? What goals for this year will move me closest to that vision?*

- *Do I really want this goal, or is it just something I think I'm supposed to want or have been told I need?* (My friend, if you're considering going to college please ponder this one well.)

- *What excites me?* (If nothing has excited you in a while, then ask what used to excite you.)

- *What scares me?* (Fear can sometimes be a place to look for goals, too.)
- *If I had all the money in the world, what would I do this year?* (Take note: The answer to this question may reveal some exciting clues for goals you may not have considered.)
- *Where am I aiming too low in life?*
- *Where am I selling myself short?*
- *Where am I settling?*
- *What no longer brings me joy?*
- *Where do I feel stuck?*
- *What am I avoiding?*
- *What am I afraid to admit?*
- *What goal is my fear trying to hide?*
- *What dream did I let die? How can I resurrect it?*
- *What skills and talents have I let lay fallow? How can I cultivate them again?*
- *How much/what am I willing to sacrifice for this goal?*

One often overlooked part of living the goal achiever's life is recognizing and admitting when a goal simply doesn't satisfy or serve us. Perhaps we've outgrown it. Or maybe it was never right for us in the first place, and we just needed to figure that out.

Another often overlooked part of living the goal achiever's life is accepting that it's sometimes okay to be uncertain about our goals. It's just not okay to use that as an excuse for doing nothing at all.

The above questions should help you find clarity in either case. If you're still unsure about what goals you want, just make the best choice you can for now. Try some goals out, and if down the road you find one or more of them aren't for you, then retire them and try some other goals on for size.

This is called *prototyping*, and it's how most great innovations come about. It's an entirely legitimate approach for innovating or reinventing your life, too. We'll talk more about prototyping in *Part 4*.

* * *

We started with a panorama of dreams and then narrowed our focus to the one-year plan. Now let's zoom into the month, the primary time-frame for planning and achieving our goals.

CHAPTER 10

Plan Your Month

The only person you are destined to become is the person you decide to be.

— RALPH WALDO EMERSON

A T THIS STAGE, many goal planning methodologies ask you to take your goals for the year and plan out every month in advance. But that's a needlessly complicated (and ineffective) waste of time. Which is why we're going to take a different approach and focus on one month at a time.

THE GOAL BUFFET METHOD

Think of your annual goal list like a buffet filled with a delicious selection of all the wonderful things you want to accomplish by year's end. At the start of every month you head over to that one-year goal buffet and load your plate up with whatever goals look tastiest. You chow down on those goals for thirty or so days, and at the start of the next month you head back to the buffet to load your plate with some more goals.

That's how we're going to approach monthly goal planning. Like little goal piggies.

HOW TO PLAN EACH MONTH

Monthly planning is best done either on the first day of the month or the last day of the previous month. Though creating a one-month plan is rarely as messy as creating a one-year plan, I often do a rough draft first and advise the same for you.

The format for monthly planning mirrors that for yearly planning, though the recommended order of some steps differs slightly.

Please don't be intimidated by the fact that there are seven steps here. This is just to help you get a clear sense of the process. Once you have a couple months of planning under your belt, they will all flow easily and intuitively together. You'll probably end up modifying them to suit your own unique needs and personal planning style, too.

Step 1: List Your Domains

Following the same format you used for your one-year goals, write down your domains and under each create a numbered list, from one through five.

Step 2: Assign Your Habit Goals

Assign any habit goals you're working on to their appropriate domains. Remember to use the *20/30 Rule* when setting the habit goal. As in, "Walk 20/30 Days."

It's best to start with habit goals because they tend to remain the same across many months, making them the easiest way to get the goal-ball rolling. All the more if you, like me, are sometimes intimidated by a blank page and just don't know where to start. Start with your habits.

Step 3: Affix True Deadlines

Transfer any goals from your one-year list that have a true deadline for this month. If you like, turn to the week and then day of the deadline in your goal journal or planner and add it there now, too.

Step 4: Transfer Incompletes

You can skip this for your first time planning, but every month hereafter . . .

Review last month's goal list for any incomplete goals. Ask yourself if this goal is still relevant and something you want to continue working on.

If it is, then transfer it to the appropriate domain on this month's list.

If it's not, let it go. This is best accomplished by playing a sappy swan song by Edith Piaf while imagining your beloved goal departing on a steamer bound for New York as you wave a handkerchief and tearfully shout, *adieu doux rêve, adieu!* (Farewell, my dream! Farewell!).

Joking.

Or am I?

Step 5: Pull From Your One-Year And Projects Lists

Review your one-year goals list. Choose what one-year goals you want to focus on this month. If a one-year goal has multiple steps, check your *Project* page and choose one or more milestones to focus on instead.

This is also a good time to do an M from *SMART* check and make sure all your goals for the year still feel meaningful. Strike out any that aren't. Never feel like this is a failure. It is simply a matter of adapting and being clear about your priorities.

Again: Edith Piaf. Handkerchief. *Adieu.*

Step 6: Choose Your Breakthrough Goals For The Month

Choose the top three goals that you'd like to achieve or make significant progress on this month. These are your one-month breakthrough goals.

Your breakthrough goals are the real focus of the month and outweigh all the other goals on your list. So much so that if you fell short on all your other goals but achieved even one breakthrough goal, you should feel like a conqueror.

Highlight your three breakthrough goals. Make them stand out on the page, like a north star that you never lose sight of as you plan each week and each day.

Often a one-month breakthrough goal will be a milestone for an annual breakthrough goal. But it doesn't have to be, either. Back to my tee shirt side-business example: Selling tees was never one of my one-year breakthrough goals, but I still made it a breakthrough goal for the month I worked on it.

Step 7: Review And Finalize Your Plan

You now have the outline of a goaltastic plan for the month. But before transferring the final version to your goal journal or planner, give it a once-over, looking for potential conflicts or oversights.

Things to consider:

- Think about the expenditure of time your goals will require and if you can commit the time necessary.
- Make sure you're not trying to cram too many one-year goals into a single month.
- Include some easy win goals. Your breakthrough goals will be challenging, so some easy wins along the way can help keep you motivated.

* * *

Are you starting to see the method to my madness? The year plan flows smoothly into the month plan, and visa versa. And the more we focus in, the more intuitive the process becomes.

Now let's zoom in on your weekly and daily plans.

CHAPTER 11

Plan Your Week And Day

I don't count the days, I make the days count!

— MUHAMMAD ALI

GOOD NEWS! Your weekly and daily planning follow the same basic pattern as planning your year and month, so I've combined instructions for both into a single chapter. These steps will quickly become second nature to you.

WEEKLY PLANNING STEPS

Plan your week Sunday evening or Monday morning using these steps:

Step 1: Create a one-week goal list, divided by domain.

Step 2: Affix any true deadlines for the week.

Step 3: Assign your habit goals (Remember to use The 5/7 Rule).

Step 4: Transfer incompletes from last week.

Step 5: Pull goals from your one-month and project lists. Assign whatever goals/milestones from each that you want to work on this week.

Step 6: Choose three breakthrough goals for the week. Your weekly breakthrough goals may or may not be the same as your monthly breakthrough goals. They could be milestones or steps towards a breakthrough goal for the month. Or they could be entirely unrelated to one-month breakthrough goals. In short, if you decide something is a breakthrough goal for the week, then that's precisely what it is.

Step 7: Review and finalize your plan.

DAILY PLANNING STEPS

Daily planning follows the now familiar pattern, with some minor differences. One of these is that you don't need to divide it into domains. For daily planning, that's overkill. So instead, I differentiate between goals of different domains by using different colored pens for each.

Step 1: List your habit goals for the day. Note that there's no equivalent to the 20/30 or 5/7 rules on your daily plan. Instead, it's strictly binary: goal achieved or not achieved.

Step 2: Write down and highlight any true deadlines. Note that on *daily planning* *a true deadline becomes an automatic breakthrough goal.*

Step 3: Transfer incompletes from yesterday.

Step 4: Review your week list. If you'd like to tackle any goals from your one-week list today, assign them.

Step 5: Choose today's breakthrough goals. Highlight or put a star next to your three most important goals for the day. Remember to include true deadlines since these are automatic breakthrough goals.

Step 6: Create Time Blocks. This is where daily planning most differs from weekly, monthly, and yearly planning. It's during the sixteen or so hours of each waking day that your boots are on the ground of goal achievement, so it's here that you need to commit time to doing the work. The best way to do this is through time blocking.

How To Time Block

To time block, decide how much time you want to commit to each domain or project, then assign blocks of time to them on your calendar. In other words, **you don't need to time block for each individual goal, just for the domain or project to which they belong.**

As a rule of thumb, each time block should be no less than thirty minutes.

As another rule of thumb, a few large time blocks of the same domain are better than numerous smaller ones spread throughout the day.

For example, my *Personal Development* goals for today include *Affirmations, Visualizations, Meditation/Japa, Walking, Journaling,* and *Reading.* Having six different *Personal Development* time blocks scattered throughout the day would defeat the purpose of time blocking. Instead, I typically consolidate my disciplines into two blocks: One in the early afternoon for *Affirmations, Visualizations, Meditation, and Walking.* Another in the evening for *Journaling* and *Reading.* Both blocks are simply labeled "PD" for *Personal Development,* so I don't have to write out each discipline.

Refer to *Resources 1* for an example of time blocking on a daily planning page.

HABIT TRACKING

As you've seen, *Breakthrough Goals!* approaches habits in a unique way by converting them into habit goals. On your daily plan, these are written down and treated like any other goal. By day's end, you've either achieved the habit goal, or you haven't.

While you should write down each of your habit goals every day, you can also use a monthly habit tracker if you like. Doing this gives you a good view of your long-term progress, like an establishing shot specifically for habits.

* * *

You now have a framework for planning your goals efficiently and effectively. To stay on track with your plan you need to review your progress regularly. That brings us to the final step in goal planning . . .

CHAPTER 12

Progress Reviews

If one advances confidently in the direction of his dreams, and endeavors to live the life which he has imagined, he will meet with a success unexpected in common hours.

— HENRY DAVID THOREAU

YOU NOW HAVE A GOAL PLAN that will guide you day by day, week by week, month by month, and year by year to a life of phenomenal success across multiple life domains. By doing this, you've made a huge leap towards creating your breakthrough life. Exciting stuff!

Now you just need to work the plan so it can work its magic on your life. This includes consistent planning, of course. But it also means doing progress reviews at the end of each day, week, month, and year to make sure you're always on the right track. Namely, the track to *success*.

DAILY REVIEW

This end-of-day review can take as little as five minutes. Review the goals you set for today and consider exploring the following questions in your goal journal.

- *What's my overall grade/score for today?*
- *What were my biggest victories today?*
- *What made me happy today? What am I grateful for?*
- *What did I fail to accomplish today, and why? (Note any valuable lessons you've learned)*
- *What one thing can I do to make tomorrow great?*
- *Additional Notes/Thoughts/Pondering*

Until recently, I preferred planning first thing in the morning. It allowed me time to ease into the day while working up excitement for what I planned to accomplish. It also lets me start the day with a quick and easy win, since planning is one of my daily disciplines.

Now I prefer reviewing my day and planning the following day at the same time, in the evening. That way I can jump right into writing after I wake up.

Both evening and morning approaches work equally well. Pick whichever one appeals most to you. Just be consistent with it.

WEEKLY REVIEW

At the end of every week, review your progress in your goal journal. You can do this in as little as ten minutes. You may want to answer some of the questions below as part of your weekly review.

- *What's my overall grade/score for the week?*
- *What are my grades/scores for each domain?*
- *What were my biggest victories this week?*
- *What made me happy this week? What am I grateful for?*
- *What did I fail to accomplish this week, and why? (Summarize any lessons you've learned)*
- *What one thing can I do to make next week great?*
- *Where did I underestimate or overestimate the time cost of a specific project or goal?*
- *Additional Notes/Thoughts/Ponderings.*

I advise planning next week immediately after reviewing the current week. Before long, weekly reviews and planning will merge into a seamless process that will take you about twenty to thirty minutes.

MONTHLY REVIEW

Do your monthly review on the last or first day of each month. I recommend investing a solid thirty minutes or more into your monthly review. I also recommend creating your new one-month plan immediately after the review.

Here are some monthly review questions you can explore in your goal journal:

- *What are my grades/scores for each domain?*

- *What's my overall grade/score for the month?*
- *What were my top victories this month?*
- *What made me happiest this month? What am I grateful for?*
- *What did I fail to accomplish this month, and why? (Summarize any lessons you have learned)*
- *What one thing can I do to make next month great?*
- *Additional Notes/Thoughts/Ponderings.*

ANNUAL REVIEW

Do your annual review on December 31st or January 1st. (Or on your birthday, if you're dividing the year that way.) I recommend investing at least an hour into your annual review. As with the monthly and weekly reviews, you should create your plan for the coming year immediately after your review of the past year.

Here are some questions to explore as part of your annual review:

- *What breakthrough goals did I achieve?*
- *What were my other successes and accomplishments in each domain?*
- *What are my grades/scores across each domain this year?*
- *What's my overall grade/score for the year?*
- *What were some happiness highlights for the year? What am I most grateful for?*
- *What did I fail to accomplish this year, and why? (Summarize any lessons you've learned)*

- *What one thing can I do to make next year great?*

- *If I were to describe this year in one word, what would it be?*

- *Additional Notes/Thoughts/Ponderings*

* * *

And that's the *Breakthrough Goals!* system. You now have a framework for planning and pursuing your goals efficiently and effectively. But we both know that's not enough. Having a great goal plan is the essential foundation for your breakthrough life, but the real work (and fun) is in the actual *building* of that life.

Part 4 is all about that.

But first, a quick review of what we've learned so far ...

Part 3 Takeaways

It's not who you are that holds you back, it's who you think you're not.

— DENIS WAITLEY

1. Create a *Dreamlist*

Capture every dream and goal that comes to you. Big ones, small ones, rational ones, and wildly fantastical ones. Free yourself to be a visionary on your *Dreamlist* and keep adding to it over time.

2. Create your one-year plan

Your establishing shot . . .

Step 1: List your domains.

Step 2: Transfer unfinished goals from last year.

Step 3: Choose goals from your *Dreamlist*.

Step 4: Define your milestones (as needed).

Step 5: Note true deadlines, run a *SMART* test, and apply *The 240 Rule*.

Step 6: Choose three breakthrough goals for the year.

Step 7: Review, edit, and finalize your plan.

When planning your year . . .

✓ It's okay to trade off goals between domains. Just **don't exceed forty total goals for the year, and don't drop below three goals in any given domain.**

✓ **Ask if your current lifestyle aligns with your goals.** If it doesn't, you may need to modify your lifestyle or your plan to create better alignment.

✓ **If you're not sure about a goal, don't be afraid to try it out for a while and see where it goes.** Pay special attention to *Chapter 26* on *Prototyping.*

3. Plan your month

Focusing in from your one-year plan . . .

Step 1: List your domains.

Step 2: Assign your habit goals. Use *The 20/30 Rule.*

Step 3: Affix any true deadlines.

Step 4: Transfer incompletes.

Step 5: Pull from your one-year goal list and project lists.

Step 6: Choose your breakthrough goals for the month.

Step 7: Review and finalize your plan.

4. Plan each week

Focusing in from your one-month plan . . .

Step 1: List your domains.

Step 2: Affix true deadlines.

Step 3: Assign habit goals using *The 5/7 Rule.*

Step 4: Transfer incompletes from last week.

Step 5: Pull from your monthly goals and projects lists.

Step 6: Choose your breakthrough goals for the week.

Step 7: Review and finalize your plan.

5. Plan each day

Focusing in from your one week plan . . .

Step 1: List your habit goals for the day.

Step 2: Highlight any true deadline goals.

Step 3: Transfer Incompletes from yesterday.

Step 4: Review your week list.

Step 5: Choose today's breakthrough goals.

Step 6: Create time blocks.

6. Do progress reviews

Each day, week, month, and year.

7. Remember the following rules of thumb:

✓ **The Goldilocks Zone is to have 3-5 goals in each domain.**

✓ **Time Blocks should be at least 30 minutes long.** Having a few bigger time-blocks is often better than having a bunch of smaller ones.

✓ When planning your year, month, week, and days aim to **include some challenging stretch goals and some easy-win goals.**

PART 4
Achieving Your Goals

To reach a port, we must sail—Sail, not tie at anchor—Sail, not drift.
— FRANKLIN D. ROOSEVELT

HAVING A PLAN IS JUST THE START of your adventure in creating a breakthrough life. It will, as I've said, put you miles ahead of most folks who passively let life happen to them rather than deliberately, mindfully, make life work for them.

But it's only the beginning.

You will face challenges, setbacks, delays, and upsets. That too is life.

I want to equip you to navigate every challenge and overcome every obstacle, skillfully.

I want you to achieve the goals you've set.

I want you to win.

So here's a large toolbox of strategies and tips to help assure that happens. They have served me well, and I'm confident they will do the same for you.

CHAPTER 13

Know Your Enemy

Rule of thumb: The more important a call or action is to our soul's evolution, the more Resistance we will feel towards pursuing it.

— STEVEN PRESSFIELD

IN THE WAR OF ART, Steven Pressfield calls "Resistance" the greatest enemy of writers and artists. I'd go further and say that it's quite possibly the greatest enemy of anyone pursuing any goal.

What is Resistance? In a nutshell, it is that part of you characterized by fear of failure, avoidance, and sometimes just downright laziness. It's the immature aspect of your psyche that avoids doing what needs to be done, even as it makes quite mature, reasonable-sounding excuses for your avoidance.

Be warned: Some of what I say in this chapter may raise your hackles. If that happens, please know that this too is Resistance at work. "Who the hell does this guy think he is? He's SO wrong. What a jerk! I'm not reading another word!"

Heeding Resistance here would be self-defeating.

So, disagree with me, if you like. Curse me in the margins, if that helps. But please keep reading with an open mind. I, too, resisted and resented some of these ideas at first. This is some tough-love medicine for the mind and ego. It may taste bad, but it heals.

With that caveat, here are some of the most familiar and nefarious manifestations of Resistance:

PROCRASTINATION. If we're honest, procrastination is just laziness dolled up as an excuse. That excuse is always the same: "I'll do it later." If you scratch just below the surface of procrastination (or laziness), you'll discover ...

"NOT FEELING LIKE IT." This is a subtle and devious form of Resistance that artists, writers, and other creative types are especially susceptible to. We have convinced ourselves that if we don't feel motivated or feel inspired to do something, then that's a reason not to do it. Which is silly. More on this later.

BRIGHT SHINY OBJECT SYNDROME. Constantly dropping perfectly good goals for new and "better" goals. The result is that we're always starting and rarely finishing. More on this later, too.

ENTITLEMENT. This form of Resistance is now epidemic. It denies personal responsibility with the conscious or unconscious belief that life, parents, society, government, the rich, or anyone other than ourselves somehow owe us security, success, health, wealth, you name it. They don't.

BLAME-GAMING. This is a particularly childish and acute form of entitlement that blames externalities for our own life outcomes. Another name for it is "Victimitus," where we define ourselves as victims of others, groups, races, parents, institutions, systems, circumstances, or fate and then use that as a handy excuse for staying stuck in life. Unfortunately, this too is now epidemic.

KING BABY. Psychologists call it "Low Frustration Tolerance." The folks in AA call it "King Baby," which I think is a great metaphor. King Baby is characterized by a childish demand that success be easier and life let us have our way. Why? Just because we say so.

At its worst King Baby is the entitlement of a foot-stomping toddler who wants what he wants when he wants it, *right now.* At its best, King Baby refuses to pursue a goal, pouting that it's "just too hard." This is just another, less honest, way of saying, "Reality should change because I say so, and if it doesn't change, then I won't play with it anymore!"

"SHOULD" AND "SHOULDN'T." These are tied for Resistance's third favorite word. Should and shouldn't are sneaky forms of Resistance because we know that, in a way, they are true.

We *should* stick with it.

We *shouldn't* procrastinate.

We *should* do the work that needs to be done.

We *shouldn't* make more excuses.

We *should* finish this chapter.

We *shouldn't* take a quick break to kill videogame zombies.

No, really. I want to kill zombies. Just fifteen minutes, twenty tops.

FFS, *No!* You should just finish writing the damn chapter!

Jeesh. Okay, *me.* Take a chill pill or something.

The problem is that beating ourselves over the head with all our shoulds—however true they may be—can be counterproductive. We hate being reminded of the obvious, and we resent being bossed around. Even when the boss doing the bossing is ourselves.

The jerk.

Should and shouldn't sap the fun from our work by framing goals as duties and exciting opportunities into burdensome obligations.

"BUT . . ." This is Resistance's second favorite word. It's always followed by a plausible justification for excusing us from doing what needs to be done. The tragic thing about such arguments against our own potential is that we always win them, which really means we always lose. As Jonathan Livingston Seagull taught us, "Argue for your limitations, and sure enough they're yours."

"CAN'T" is Resistance's very favorite word. Where But is an argument for our limitations, Can't is what happens once you've won that argument and lost a bit of authenticity in the process. Can't is surrender, acquiescence, and—I'm just going to say it—cowardice.

Take courage: Can't is almost always a lie. As you will discover, you almost always certainly *Can.*

These are by no means the only manifestations of Resistance, but they are the most common. Guard against them because the first step in defeating Resistance is seeing through its disguises and recognizing when it's trying to bewitch you with its diabolical magic.

Exercise: Spotting Resistance

Think of a recent important goal that you started but failed to finish. Reflect on the thoughts and feelings you had at the time you gave up. What form or forms did Resistance take?

- Was it simply an issue of procrastination or laziness dressed up with the excuse that you'll get to it later?

- Did you stop feeling motivated or inspired, and just give up?

- Did *Bright Shiny Object Syndrome* seduce you into starting on a new and "better" goal before finishing what you'd started?

- Did you fail to start or finish a goal because, at some level, you felt entitled to success without having to put in the necessary effort?

- Did you blame others (people, systems, groups, government, Capitalism, bigotry, bias, the weather, whatever) for why you failed to start or stick with a goal?

- Did you have a King Baby moment and stop playing because life refused to bend to your demand that it be easier?

- Did you burden yourself with a bunch of unhelpful *shoulds* and shouldn'ts that undermined the joy of your goal, causing you to give up on it?
- Did you argue for your own limitations with a bunch of *buts* and win that self-defeating argument with some *cants*?

Repeat this exercise a couple more times with important goals that you either never started or failed to finish. When it comes to disrupting your goals, Resistance, paradoxically, prefers the path of least resistance. If it finds a strategy that works, it will repeat that strategy over and over again. So look for triggers and patterns. Becoming aware of them is the first step to overcoming them. Know your enemy.

* * *

Merely recognizing Resistance isn't enough, of course. The goal is to defeat it. All of the conceptual tools in the rest of *Part 4* will help you do just that. But since "I feel like it" is such an extra-slippery form of Resistance, let's dig deeper into that one.

CHAPTER 14

Goals Don't Care About Your Feelings

Of course motivation is not permanent. But then neither is bathing, but it is something you should do on a regular basis.

— ZIG ZIGLAR

A S A WRITER, I've had my share of writer's block. It was my go-to excuse for not finishing blog posts, articles, or books. But that all began to change after reading this line from Larry Kahaner:

> *I don't believe in writers' block. Do doctors have "doctors block?" Do plumbers have "plumbers" block?' No. We all have days when we don't feel like working, but why do writers turn that into something so damn special by giving it a faintly romantic name?*

It's true. Many writers and artists embrace the comforting mythology that our work comes only when the fickle Muses decide to bless us with inspiration. But if you look at the most prolific writers and artists in history, that is simply not the case.

They sat down, day in and day out, and worked. Only then did inspiration come.

Sometimes.

If they were lucky.

But inspired or not, lucky or not, they wrote.

As Stephen King said, "Amateurs sit and wait for inspiration, the rest of us just get up and go to work."

And as Woody Allen said, "Eighty percent of success is showing up."

This lesson applies to everyone with goals, not just writers. One of the biggest myths we tell ourselves is that how we feel determines what we can do.

It doesn't.

We say, "I just don't feel motivated to work out today." As if that somehow has any bearing whatsoever on whether or not we **can** work out.

Author and podcaster Ben Shapiro likes to say, "Facts don't care about your feelings." One of those facts is that our goals don't care about our feelings either. Both the fact that I'm thirty pounds overweight and my goal to lose that weight are deaf to my protest: "But I don't *feel* like exercising! I want to watch reruns of the Golden Girls while eating cheesecake!"

"Picture it. Sicily. 1948. Doesn't matter if you feel like it. You're fat. Put down the cheesecake and go to the gym."

The truth is that we do things we don't feel motivated to do every single day. If we didn't, we wouldn't be functioning human beings in the world. We get up and go to work on days when we'd rather stay in bed. We do our dishes, we make our beds, and we tidy up when it would be so much easier to be slobs. We smile, say thank you, and usually try to be civil to others—even when we're irritated or stressed.

It's only with important things like goals that we suddenly imagine that feeling motivated is a prerequisite to doing what needs to be done. And that is a tell-tale sign that Resistance is at work on us.

ACTION PRECEDES MOTIVATION

Nine times out of ten, action precedes motivation, not the other way around. First, you sit your ass down and start writing because that's what you promised yourself you'd do. Only then, after a few go-nowhere sentences (or paragraphs), do you find your figurative stride and want to finish the whole chapter.

Action first, motivation second.

You reluctantly step on the treadmill, and it's only after a tedious two miles that you find your literal and figurative stride, the endorphins start flowing, and you remember how much you love running.

Action first, motivation second.

You look at the three-page checklist of things you need to learn about and do to start your own home business. It's overwhelming, and you want to procrastinate, but you don't. Instead, you pick something easy: "Brainstorm biz name." This leads to you finding the perfect business name. And that leads to checking off another item from the list: "Buy domain name."

You're on a roll, so you go ahead and buy hosting, too, and start working on yet another task from the list: "Build website."

Action first, motivation second.

Nothing is more motivating than success. So take action now and, more often than not, the good feelings will follow.

Doing What It Takes

And what if feeling motivated doesn't follow taking action?

So what.

A goal remains the goal, irrespective of our fickle moods. On sunny days and stormy days. On days we feel great and on days we feel like garbage. Some days we need to smile our way through to success. And others, we need to tell our feelings to shut the hell up, clench our jaws, and muscle through.

Our goals reflect our best selves working to create our best lives. So ultimately, we do the work because it needs to be done, it deserves to be done, and because no one else can do it. We do the work in faith that the burden we feel in doing the work today will be made light in the joy we will feel in success tomorrow. This refusal to put our long-term goals at the mercy of fleeting feelings proves that we have what it takes to succeed.

MOTIVATION BREWING INSTRUCTIONS

Some people treat their morning coffee as a necessary essential. For me, it is an advantageous non-essential. I don't need it to wake up and get to work writing each morning, but it sure does help. The same goes for motivation. It's not essential, but it sure is nice to start the day with a big steaming mug of it, extra cream, hold the sugar. Just getting to work does this, as we've talked about already. Here are some other ways to brew motivation.

Create A Routine

If you have a routine in place that gets you moving without even having to think about it, then you don't have to think about whether or not you're feeling motivated. You start working on autopilot and before long motivation kicks in. *Chapter 22, Create Rules, Rituals, And Systems* has some ideas you should find helpful for creating routines.

Get Some Quick And Easy Wins

What we call a lack of motivation is very often fear in disguise. When the sheer scope of a goal intimidates you into indecision or inaction, start with something easy and give yourself a quick win.

Recently my weight loss hit a wall. I won't point the finger at binging on *The Golden Girls* and cheesecake, but it was *The Golden Girls* and cheesecake. In any case, losing weight is an emotionally weighty goal for me, so I started small. "Research top diet programs + Choose One." It took about twenty minutes to read a few reviews, pick the best option, and sign up. (In case you're wondering, it was *Weight Watchers*).

Start small. Start easy. Give yourself a few quick wins. This will encourage you and fuel your motivation.

Tackle The Big Scary Goal

You can also take the exact opposite approach and start with one giant, intimidating goal. Conquering a big scary goal will make you feel powerful. And feeling powerful is powerfully motivating. You'll want to ride that momentum and knock out more goals since they will seem easy by comparison.

Just be careful with this approach. If you're still too reliant on feeling motivated to do your work, then tackling the big scary goal too soon may be unwise. Failure could feel devastating. First, get some experience doing your work irrespective of how you feel. Build a routine, or start small, like in the previous tip. Then, once you feel a bit more confident, take on the big scary goal.

Change Your State

You can change your emotional state by changing your physical state. If, for example, you want to feel motivated, then sit up straight, pull your shoulders back, and smile with enthusiasm.

When I'm on a writing roll my knee sometimes bounces with nervous excitement (and probably caffeine). So when not feeling motivated, I may bounce my knee as if I was nervously excited (and caffeinated). This tricks my mind into making me feel motivated.

Set A Timer

Some people do their best work when the pressure is on. If that's you, then by all means leverage that for motivation. Make a game of it by setting a timer and trying to beat the bell.

Find Your Why

This one is so important that I've dedicated an entire chapter to it. That's next.

CHAPTER 15

Where There's A Will There's A Why

He who has a why to live for can bear with almost any how.

— NIETZSCHE

THE BIGGER YOUR GOAL, the more challenges you'll likely face on the path to achieving that goal. When this happens, Resistance will try to manipulate you with a litany of reasons for why you should give up . . .

It's just too hard.
I'm not smart enough.
I'm not strong enough.
I'm not good enough.
I don't have what it takes.
Maybe this is a sign that I should give up.
The odds are stacked too high against me.
Prejudice is holding me back.
What was I thinking? I'll never succeed at this.
Maybe now isn't a good time for it.

I need to be more practical.

I should have gone with Plan B.

I need to deal with this crisis. Then I'll get back to the goal.

I deserve a break.

Screw it.

You've already created one tool designed to help weather these assaults on your resolve to win: An inspired vision of your ideal future. This can carry you far.

Yet, Resistance is relentless. It may throw such huge obstacles in our way that we lose faith in our visualized ideal future and raise the white flag of surrender. Arguably worse is the "Chinese water torture" approach where it seems like individually minor setbacks just won't stop coming . . . Drip, drip, drip, setback, setback, setback . . . as our resolve is slowly worn away, and the cumulative pain becomes so great that we finally give up.

The term "lose heart" is apt here. What, after all, remains to keep us going when our heart is no longer in the fight?

One thing and one thing only. **Sheer force of Will.**

WILLPOWER

Over the last few years a trend in personal development literature has been to poo-poo the importance of Willpower in achieving our goals. I'm going to let you in on a little secret: It's all a marketing ploy. More bluntly, a lie. Telling folks that a weak Will is one reason their life is crap doesn't sell books. Telling people, "It's not your fault! Willpower is a myth! There's an easier way . . ." *That* sells.

Especially now, when a historically unprecedented number of adults are too emotionally immature and fragile to deal with delay, setback, criticism, or not getting their way. In a word, adulthood. In another word, life.

If you want to achieve your goals, you need to leave that delicate and complacent herd and reclaim your individual Willpower.

The Alchemy Of Willpower

Willpower comes from an alliance of heart and mind. It's the emotional desire for success buttressed with a good reason to succeed, a **why**. So, to increase Willpower you need to get clear on why your goal is important and why you're committed to achieving it. This will steel your resolve to push through any disappointment, discouragement, fear, doubt, or setback you encounter.

Here's a motto for you: *Your Why is why you Will.*

Getting clear on your Why is a good litmus test for determining if a goal is relevant and meaningful, too. When your heart sings for a goal, it's usually easy to find your whys. Whereas if you struggle to find a good why, there's a good chance the goal isn't really meaningful to you. You may want to ask yourself if it's truly your goal or one that you just think you're supposed to have.

Exercise: Finding Your Why

Find your why by reflecting on questions like these in your goal journal:

- Why do I want to achieve this goal? Why is it important/what makes it meaningful to me?

- Why is it important that I do this *now*? (This is a good one if you've been procrastinating on a goal).

- What excites me about this goal?

- What are my top five reasons for wanting this change?

- What are five ways that success here will improve my life?

- How will I feel about myself and my life once I achieve this goal?

- How will I feel if I give up on or fail at this goal?

- What am I losing every day by *not* pursuing this goal?

- What will happen if I *don't* change now and keep going down the road I'm on? (A powerful and often uncomfortable question for using pain to get leverage on yourself).

You don't need to list whys for every single goal you set, but at least do it with your annual breakthrough goals.

* * *

Now that you are armed with some powerful whys to strengthen your Willpower and sustain you through challenges and setbacks, let's talk more about your single greatest success ally: Your own mind.

CHAPTER 16

Change Your Mind

If you think you can do a thing or think you can't do a thing, you're right.

— HENRY FORD

YOUR THOUGHTS CREATE YOUR REALITY. It's an old and storied idea. Medieval occultists believed a version of it. Modern Cognitive-Behavioral Therapists, too. New Agers and spiritual non-conformists call it "the Secret." Show me the money pragmatists and just the facts mam realists call it "common sense." Even some renegade scientists are getting on board with the idea, risky as that is.

Some people believe it describes a metaphysical fact of the universe and that our mind has the literal power to leverage material reality for manifesting our desires through mechanisms we don't yet fully understand.

Others prefer a more down-to-earth argument, which simply points out that by mastering our thoughts, we master ourselves. And by mastering ourselves, we master the circumstances of our lives.

"All that we are is the result of what we have thought," said the Buddha.

"What things soever ye desire, when ye pray, believe that ye receive them, and ye shall have them," said Jesus (Mark 11:24).

"As above, so below. As within, so without," says The Emerald Tablet of Hermeticism.

"Every thought is a cause, and every condition is an effect. Change your thoughts and you change your destiny," said New Thought minister and author, Joseph Murphy.

"When the individual mind touches the Universal Mind, it receives all its power," said another New Thought pioneer, Charles Haanel.

More pragmatically: *"You create your thoughts. Your thoughts create your intentions. Your intentions create your world,"* said motivational writer and speaker, Wayne Dyer.

It doesn't matter if you're of a metaphysical bent or more of a nuts and bolts thinker. **However you look at it, mastering our minds and marshaling our thoughts is key to achieving our goals.**

If you want to be lean, fit, and healthy, you can't maintain a mindset that views veggies with disdain and exercise as a painful chore. Instead, you must train yourself to think like someone who enjoys living a fit and healthy lifestyle.

If you want to meet the man or woman of your dreams, you must become the person who believes yourself worthy of your ideal relationship and knows that your soulmate is out there.

No matter what tools you use and support you have, you'll never beat an addiction that you don't believe can be beat.

And, short of winning the lottery, you will never get rich thinking like a poor person. Even if you did win the lottery, scarcity thinking would probably cause you to quickly squander it all.

CHANGE YOUR MIND(S)

If your thoughts create your reality, and there's something about your current reality that you don't like, then it follows that you need to change your mind about that reality. You need new positive, habitual thought patterns to replace your old negative habitual thought patterns. There are two ways to go about this: Change your critical mind, or change your subconscious mind.

Change Your Critical Mind

Your critical mind is your conscious, rational mind, or ego. It's that part, aspect, or mode (whichever you prefer) of your mind that reasons, evaluates, and analyzes. It is often also critical in the negative sense of the word, taking a grim suspicious view of the world. It can be a wet blanket on your dreams and a naysayer of your goals because it prefers to focus on all that *could* go wrong. Not because it's your enemy, but because it wants to keep you safe.

Unfortunately, this focus on safety is precisely what makes your critical mind such an easy mark for Resistance, whose forked tongue whispers apocalyptic prophecies into its ear. "If you pursue this goal, you will surely fail. You'll go bankrupt, your family and friends will abandon you, and your neighbors will point and laugh at you whenever you leave the house, which you shouldn't do anyway because it's very, very, very dangerous out there."

The way to counter the Resistance's beguiling lies is to convince your critical mind in a language it understands: *Reason.*

Exercise: Argue For The Defense

Choose a goal that you told yourself you couldn't achieve. Write down every argument you have used against that goal.

Now muster your very best counterarguments for each. Poke holes in the prosecution's claims. Be Perry Mason demolishing Hamilton Burger.

Exercise: Use Snappy Happy Technique

Our habitual negative thinking patterns can start with a single thought but then run on autopilot, spinning out entire depressing or anxiety-creating narratives that keep us from taking action on our goals. This exercise is about catching and interrupting these patterns, then replacing them with new and better ones. I call it the *Snappy Happy Technique.*

Next week, wear a rubber band on your wrist and try to catch yourself when spinning out limiting or negative narratives. Interrupt those patterns by giving yourself a snap of the rubber band. Then immediately replace the negative and limiting thought pattern with a positive and empowering alternative. Snappy. Happy.

"Oh crap, I'm going to be late for work again. I'll probably get written up this time. If I lose my job, I'm screwed—"
Snap
"I'll probably still be on time or only a little late. No big deal."

"I'm so bad with money, it's ridiculous. I just can't stick with a budget—"
Snap
"I'm learning how to manage money, easily and well."

"I'll probably die alone. I feel invisible at my age. It's not fair that—"
Snap
"There's plenty of fish in the sea. My years have given me wisdom. Plus, I look pretty damn good, actually. I'll find that perfect someone when the time is right."

"I'm such a loser—"
Snap
"I'm getting better every day."

"I can't—"
Snap
"I can. And I will."

Note: The snap is just a means of physically interrupting a mental habit. It doesn't need to be painful. Though, if you prefer a bit of sting, I guess that's fine too. Far be it from me to judge your kinky masochistic rubber band snapping lifestyle choices.

Change Your Subconscious Mind

Your critical mind thinks it's the boss, but it's not. It's the subconscious mind that pulls most of your strings. The majority of your mental processes occur at a subconscious level, which is why *only* relying on Willpower and reasoning with your critical mind isn't always sufficient to create lasting change. You need to change your subconscious mind, too.

The subconscious mind doesn't understand reason. It is the mind of dreams, imagery, and feeling. To change it, you need to speak its language. Three simple and effective ways to do this are by using *affirmations, visualizations, and hypnosis (or guided meditation)*.

Affirmations

An idea or goal can be impressed on the subconscious through repetition. You experience this with habituated behaviors all the time: you brush your teeth without thinking about it, drive your car without thinking about it, and so on. The same principle holds with developing habits of thought.

By repeating the same phrases over and over again as affirmations, you can displace old and unhelpful thought patterns and replace them with new and beneficial thought patterns.

Affirmations are most effective when they are repeated with emotion because the subconscious is fluent in feeling. Or when repeated in a drowsy, near-meditative state, because this is when your critical mind has let its guard down, giving you more direct access to the subconscious.

Exercise: Try Some Affirmations

Search online for affirmations that focus on any domain or aspect of your life you want to improve or any goal you want to achieve. Pick a couple and repeat them twenty times each, every morning (A good time for this is while showering. I call it "shower power," because I'm weird that way).

Affirmation tips:

- ✓ Write them on post-it notes and place them at various spots around the house. Whenever you see the reminder, repeat the affirmation.
- ✓ Look in the mirror when repeating affirmations. This is highly effective for affirmations dealing with self-esteem and self-worth. It may feel weird at first but push through that discomfort.
- ✓ Go for affirmation walks. Try to harmonize your affirmation with your stride.
- ✓ Repeat your affirmations just before going to bed.
- ✓ Infuse your affirmations with feeling. Repeat them with a big smile.

Visualizations

Your subconscious mind can't distinguish between an authentic and visualized experience. When you vividly imagine yourself being successful at a task, achieving a goal with ease, or living the life you aspire to live, your subconscious responds in the same way that it would if you were really practicing at the task, achieving the goal, and living that life. It will gradually shift your conscious attitudes and behaviors so that your external reality aligns with your envisioned reality.

Keep imagining yourself living a wealthy lifestyle, for example, and you will develop a wealth-oriented consciousness. This will help you see financial opportunities you'd otherwise not have noticed, while your behaviors and choices will become increasingly wealth-oriented, enabling, and generating. You will, just like the title of Napoleon Hill's classic book says, *Think and Grow Rich*.

Exercise: Visualize Your Ideal Day

Imagine that you are healthy, wealthy, and joyous in every respect. Your life is precisely how you want it to be. Now visualize yourself going through your perfect day in this perfect life, from the time you wake up to the time you lay down to go to sleep. Go through your morning, afternoon, and night. Where are you? What are you doing? Who are you with?

Viz Tips:

✓ Do this relaxed. It's best if you can get in a semi-dreamy state.

✓ Move through it. If you have a hard time seeing the scene, try moving through it in your mind. In other words, don't visualize snapshots, visualize a movie.

✓ Visualize from a first-person perspective. This one is a challenge for me. Don't visualize as if watching yourself as a character in the movie. See what happens as if you were witnessing it from your own point of view.

✓ Engage all the senses. Don't just see, but also *feel* the texture of things. *Smell* the smells. *Hear* the sounds, *Taste* the flavors. Try to engage all of your senses.

✓ Repeat. Repeat. Repeat. As with affirmations, don't just visualize once and call it a day. Visualize often—ideally, every day.

Hypnosis And Guided Meditation

The subconscious mind is sensitive to suggestions when your brain is in the drowsy Alpha or Theta states typical of hypnosis. The good news is that you don't need to learn self-hypnosis or find a professional hypnotist to take advantage of this powerful mental reprogramming method. A search on YouTube will net a myriad of guided meditation and hypnosis tracks (though of varying quality).

Exercise: Try A Guided Hypnosis

Go to YouTube. Search for hypnosis or guided meditation videos related to an area of your life you want to change. There are tons of them, though of varying quality. Try a few out, including eight-hour hypnosis tracks that you can listen to while sleeping.

You can also try out one of my recommended hypnosis/guided meditation programs in *Resources 2*.

* * *

Begin today using one or more of these tools to start displacing and replacing limiting thought patterns with positive ones.

Change your mind at the **conscious, critical level** by rationally arguing *against* your limitations and *for* your potential.

Change your mind **subconsciously** by using affirmations, visualization, and hypnosis, or guided meditation.

Saturate your mind at **both levels** with positive thoughts, optimistic thoughts, empowering thoughts, goal thoughts, success thoughts, victory thoughts.

It may take time, but if you're consistent, you will begin to notice a marked positive transformation in your outlook, your attitude, and your outcomes. The subconscious tools, especially, are like the wardrobe leading to your own inner Narnia, where magic is real. Sans the White Witch, of course.

CHAPTER 17

The Power Of Framing

Words form the thread on which we string our experiences.
— ALDOUS HUXLEY

IT WAS A SURPRISE ATTACK. Now, some twenty-five thousand U.S. Marines were encircled by over one-hundred and twenty thousand Chinese infantry. Supplies were dwindling. And to make already terrible matters worse, it was the coldest winter Korea had seen in a hundred years. Here's how Colonel Chesty Puller, commander of the 1st Marines, summed up the situation: "We've been searching for the enemy. The problem is now solved. We're surrounded."

What followed was one of the most harrowing and heroic episodes of the Korean war. Under relentless fire, the beleaguered Marines punched their way through enemy lines, mile by mile, hill by hill, carrying their wounded and dead over a thirty-five-mile gauntlet of hell.

When asked about the Marines' retreat, General O.P. Smith famously answered, "Retreat, hell! We're attacking in a different direction!"

Colonel Puller and General Smith weren't just dealing out witty, ballsy bravado here (Though that too, and impressively). They understood that we can't always control circumstances, but we can always control how we interpret those circumstances. In other words, they understood the importance of *framing*.

Framing is the meaning with which we clothe experience, and it can be the deciding factor in whether or not we end up the victims of fate or the masters of it.

There are three areas where framing is essential: In how we define our past failures; in how we define our current challenges; and in how we define our bad habits.

(RE)FRAMING "FAILURES" AND CURRENT CHALLENGES

The goal gods, it seems, like to test our faith, courage, resolve, and ingenuity by putting obstacles on our path of goal achievement. How we frame those obstacles is important.

I'll use my goal of publishing this book as an example. A couple months ago, I published the pdf-only beta version on my website. I made a Facebook ad and was so excited when I clicked "submit," launching it into the sea of over two billion Facebook users. "Algorithms do your work. Find my people."

I ran the ad for a week.

A few thousand people saw it.

A few dozen clicked on it.

No one bought it.

Gut-punch.

There are any number of negative ways I could have famed this fail. I could have decided it meant . . .

- I'll never succeed as a writer.
- All that work was for nothing.
- I'm delusional. My goal system is actually stupid.
- I'm old. They just want to use apps.
- No one wants to take responsibility for their lives anymore.
- This is unfair.
- This is BS.
- Facebook's algorithms suck.
- God is being a jerk.

I confess that Resistance briefly tempted me with some of these negative frames. It's only natural to question yourself and doubt your course after working hard on an important goal only to hit a wall.

But after a couple of days of self-pity, I put down the Tillamook Chocolate Peanut Butter ice cream, turned off Netflix, straightened my back, clenched my jaw, looked in the figurative mirror, and in the voice of a stereotypical British First Lieutenant from the Great War said: "Chin up, old boy! Enough of this sad sack dilly-dallying. The fight isn't over yet, by God! Time to get back to it and give that Kaiser the what for!"

I chose to assign new meanings to the setback by re-framing it. In my head, the process went something like this:

My goal was to publish by next month. So I actually achieved the goal early. Let's just consider this my "beta" launch. It's an opportunity to work out the kinks and have a second, better, launch.

...and...

If no one bought the book, then no one read the book. If no one read the book, then no one could hate the book. So Resistance can shut up with its "'the book sucks!" nonsense.

...and...

This fail probably means my website or ad messaging sucks. I can improve those.

A consciousness shift happens once you get on a positive reframing roll, and you start to see all the **opportunities in the apparent failure:**

This is an opportunity to improve a couple of chapters that felt a bit off to me.

I wanted to have more quotes in the book. Now I have time to find and add some great ones.

I wasn't delighted with the formatting and overall aesthetic. Now I can polish that before the real launch.

This is perfect because I can now have Kindle and print versions finished for the real launch, too. That's big.

I'm glad I had this setback now rather than later.

God is guiding me to victory. He knows the best route, even when I don't. Keep the faith. Keep on. I got this.

Napoleon Hill said, "In every failure is the seed of its equivalent success." It's true. We find that seed by reframing the apparent failure into a mere setback, a stumble, a trip-up on the path. Consider the difference between these frames:

I failed. I'm such a loser. It's too hard. I'll never succeed. I might as well give up.

. . . Versus . . .

Okay, I've had a setback. My goal has been more challenging than I thought it would be. Not ideal, but that's just how it goes. The game isn't over yet—I got this!

The first frame judges, discourages, and closes off options. The second frame evaluates, affirms, and keeps options open. The first frame makes you feel like crap. The second frame makes you want to buckle down and get back to work.

As Tony Robbins says in *Awaken The Giant Within*:

The moment we place [a] mold around our experience, the label we put on it becomes our experience. What was "a bit challenging" becomes "devastating" . . . The words that we attach to our experience become our experience.

As a rule, success is cumulative; it has momentum built into it. But so too, failure. As Jack Canfield says:

You are never stuck. You just keep recreating the same experiences over and over by thinking the same thoughts, maintaining the same beliefs, speaking the same words, and doing the same things.

In other words, repeated failure is a result (at least in part) of our habitual negative framing and the meanings it creates. So, reframing our setbacks and perceived failures isn't just a feel-good exercise. It's a practical and rational exercise. **It sets your view of reality aright.**

(RE)FRAMING BAD HABITS

As the old saying goes, "An ounce of prevention is worth a pound of cure." So too with framing. By framing our goals positively at the outset, we increase our odds of achieving them and not falling prey to negative frames when obstacles arise. This is especially true when setting goals to break bad habits.

When setting a goal to break a bad habit, our instinct is to frame it negatively since we are trying to eliminate or reduce undesirable behaviors. *Don't* smoke, *don't* drink, *don't* procrastinate, *don't* back-bite. There's nothing to say you can't or won't succeed at breaking bad habits when framing them this way. But as Thomas Jefferson said, it's best to "take things always by their smooth handle." We can always swing the axe of determination to chop down bad habits, but our swings will be weaker if the handle is rough and our hands or full of splinters. A positive frame makes for a smooth handle, no splinters.

When, for example, I was working on moderating my drinking, instead of writing, "Don't drink 20/30 days," I'd write, "Stay Sober 20/30 days." Similarly, notice the difference between these formulations:

Don't eat junk food 5/7 days. **Versus** *Choose only healthy snacks 5/ 7 Days.*

Don't smoke all week. **Versus** *Remain smoke-free all week.*

Don't procrastinate after work. **Versus** *Write for 1 hour immediately after work 5/7 days.*

Don't binge on Netflix. **Versus** *Limit TV time to 2 hrs./night.*

By using positive thou shalt rather than negative thou shalt not terms, the second frame of each is more inviting and less demanding. It's human nature to welcome invitations and resent demands, even when those demands are imposed on ourselves, by ourselves.

* * *

Let's finish up this chapter with some framing and re-framing exercises.

Exercise: Reframing Past Failures

Think about one or more important goals that you've failed to achieve in the past. The more important the goal, the more likely it is that you've evolved some constricting narratives to explain your failure and justify not recommitting to the goal. Let's dismantle those narratives and replace their negative frames.

Pick a goal and write this sentence: "I failed at [name the goal] because . . ." Then finish the sentence with as many "reasons" that come to mind.

If, for example, you were writing the next *Great American Novel*, it might look like this:

I failed to finish writing my novel because . . .

- I can't figure out how to plot.
- I'm too easily distracted.
- I never finish what I start.
- I lost my job so I couldn't finish it.
- I didn't have enough time.
- My ex was a jerk.
- My dog died.
- I was too depressed.

Now reframe them to have more positive, realistic, and helpful meanings. **One way to do this is by noting where the frame is irrational and creating a rational alternative.**

- ✓ *Of course I can figure out how to plot a novel. Plotting is like any other skill and can be learned with study and mastered with practice.*
- ✓ *I can focus when I want to, and I can also learn to improve my focus.*
- ✓ *I finish things I start all the time. I can finish writing a novel too.*
- ✓ *I lost my job and chose to stop working on my novel. That wasn't a fail; it was just a poor choice and a temporary setback.*

✓ *We all have the same twenty-four hours in a day. Maybe I didn't prioritize writing as I should have. But I can choose to make better use of my time from now on.*

✓ *Yes, my ex was a jerk, my dog died, and I was depressed. These hardships made focusing on writing difficult but not impossible. I can remember that, forgive myself, and begin again.*

Exercise: Frame Current Challenges

If you're currently facing any challenges in life, open your goal journal and create some positive frames. Remember that negative frames close doors, while positive frames throw them open.

This is a temporary challenge. That's all.

This isn't the end. It's only a setback. One that I can and will overcome.

I'll find a way through, around, over, or under this obstacle.

This has been tough, but I have what it takes to win. I got this.

Well played, Resistance. But the game isn't over yet. Not even close. I. WILL. win.

Exercise: Reframe Bad Habits

Ask yourself if there are more constructive ways to frame any bad-habit-breaking goals you have. While you might not always be able to reframe bad habits, it's worth trying. Doing so may be just the edge you need to finally and forever break that bad habit.

CHAPTER 18

Grade, Gamify, And Celebrate

People rarely succeed unless they have fun in what they are doing.
— DALE CARNEGIE

HAVE SOME FUN tracking your progress and staying on target by grading, gamifying, and celebrating your days, weeks, months, and years. Here's how it works...

GRADING

Every Day: Assign a grade or score reflecting how effective you were for the day. You can use a traditional F-A+ grading system or a 1-10 scale. Whatever you prefer.

There is no hard and fast rule or rigid metric to follow here. It's best to go with how you feel about your progress. After all, we all have days that don't go according to plan but that are nevertheless outstanding. Like when you've set aside two hours to draw, but you're feeling inspired so decide to skip two other goals for the day and keep drawing until you and your Muses are exhausted. On paper, your day may look like a C+ since you only accomplished one important goal. But you know better. So you should grade it better, too. A+.

Each Week: During your weekly reviews, grade your effectiveness in each domain.

Next, grade your effectiveness for the week overall.

Alternately, you can use the simplified method and skip grading for each domain and only assign an overall grade for the week.

Each Month: Same as each week. Grade your performance by domain, then give your month an overall effectiveness grade. Or just grade the month as a whole.

Each Year: Same as above.

Why Grade?

Here are three benefits of grading:

Positive Momentum

When you've had a highly successful day and give yourself the mini-celebration of honoring it with a good grade, you'll be more likely to maintain that momentum and have another successful day tomorrow.

Negative Motivation

When you've fallen short of your expectations for the day, week, or month a low grade can motivate you to do better going forward.

This is especially true after slacking off for multiple days. When we fall into a rut of procrastination or inaction, the tendency is to bury our head in the sand and ignore how long we've been neglecting our goals. But a week of Ds and Fs is hard to ignore.

By grading each day we're forced to see the reality of where we're headed if we continue slacking off: *Nowhere*. This in turn motivates us to get back on track sooner rather than later. Pain—including the pain of failure—is unpleasant, but it can be powerful leverage.

Identifying Patterns

With a grade, it's easier to spot patterns in high and low performing days. For example, supposed you notice that on most high grade days you meditated after lunch. While on your worst-performing days, you didn't meditate at all. You can use this insight to improve your daily plan from now on.

GAMIFY

Grading shouldn't feel like a burden or a chore. Instead, have fun with it by gamifying your progress. Strive to "beat your previous score" from yesterday, last week, or last month.

Try gamifying your productivity, too. By using a free time-tracking site like Clockify.com, you can try to beat your record from yesterday or last week.

For example, if I wrote three hours yesterday, I may shoot for writing three hours and five minutes today. I'll sometimes put a half-hour block of "Flex" time in my planner right after my three-hour writing block to leave wiggle room for this kind of game. Making it "Flex" instead of just extending my writing block, defines it as an *option* instead of a goal.

This is important.

Gamifying can serve a goal but should not become a goal. There's a time for being a dutiful goal achiever, and there's a time for just having fun with it. Gamifying is always about just having fun with it.

Fuck-it Days

The bad news is time flies. The good news is that you're the pilot.
—MICHAEL ALTSHULER

When I was a raging drunk, there was a guy who I'd sometimes see at my local watering hole who found an effective way to moderate his drinking. It entailed permitting himself one glass of wine each night, along with two unplanned days each month when he could let loose, if he wanted to. He called these "*Fuck-it* days."

To me "cheat day" sounded like a failure. While "treat day" sometimes felt like a lie you tell yourself after the fact to feel better about cheating. Whereas "*Fuck-it* day" had a no-nonsense GenX feel to it. I like that. Because GenX rocks. But I digress . . .

While I had to find a different tool for addressing my own over-drinking, *Fuck-it* days have served me well in goal achievement generally, and they might do the same for you.

Earlier I talked about how "not feeling like it" is usually a cop-opt manufactured by Resistance, but sometimes it can be a legitimate sign that we need to give ourselves a break. Playing hooky on our goals for a day may be just the thing we need.

That's why having one or two *Fuck-it* days in reserve each month is a good idea. Days where you can set aside your goal plan or success routine, guilt-free, and do whatever the hell you feel like doing.

As in . . .

Yeah, I have goals I planned to work on today but Fuck-it. I'm going to spend the day in my jammies watching He-Man while feasting on a bottomless bowl of Honeycomb cereal like I did when I was a kid. I have the power!

(And, yes, I've done this. Don't judge me. You're not my real dad!).

On the other hand, you also need to be careful lest Resistance appropriate your *Fuck-it* days for its own diabolically lazy ends.

Make no mistake, it will try to do this. **Be vigilant.** Don't rush to declare a *Fuck-it* day the moment you feel like it. If you're tempted to take a *Fuck-it* a mere three days into the month, for example, Resistance is probably playing you. It's better to make a game of earning your *Fuck-it* days before spending them.

So give yourself one or two *Fuck-it* days each month, and enjoy them, guilt-free. Just try to earn them first, and make sure that when you use one it's a clear-eyed decision rather than passive acquiescence to Resistance.

CELEBRATE

Remember to celebrate your wins, too. When having a good day I give myself a word of praise. When passing an important milestone, I may treat myself to a new book. When achieving huge goals, like publishing this book, I may reward myself with a weekend mini-vacation at a fancy hotel or resort.

When celebrating a big win, take time to think about all it took to get there. Think about the obstacles you faced, the times you almost gave up but didn't, the self-doubts you refused to heed, the little victories along the way that kept you going.

This is no time for modesty.

Take pride in what you've accomplished.

Acknowledge your courage. Raise a toast to your fortitude.

Cheer your damn bullheadedness.

You worked your ass off putting your heart and soul into this goal. Celebrate it with the self-satisfaction of a Caesar staging a Triumph through Rome, or the glee of drag queen getting a fabulous new wig.

Exercise: Create A Rewards And Treats List

Start a *Rewards and Treats* list now in your goal journal. Include big and small rewards.

Pick an item from this list whenever you achieve a goal, like it's a success celebration smorgasbord!

CHAPTER 19

Expand Your Comfort Zone

I have stepped outside my Comfort Zone enough to know that, yes, the world does fall apart, but not in the way that you fear.

— TAN LE

IKE A WARM FUZZY BLANKET on a cold winter's day, the Comfort Zone is one of the most irresistible seductions of Resistance, and one of the biggest obstacles to success in life. It is only natural to do what is easy rather than what is needful, to slack off, to avoid struggle, to hide from what we fear, and to flee pain. And we are blessed to live in a pampered era where we are free to stay in the warm cocoon of our Comfort Zone indefinitely, if we choose. Most humans throughout history never had that option.

We should be grateful.

We should also be careful.

When left unchecked, Comfort Zones have a way of contracting so that our warm fuzzy blanket becomes a straightjacket. You already know this. How easy it is to turn a self-care day into a do-nothing week or a cheat day into a screw-it week.

Remember King Baby? Resistance reigns like a bratty child king over the Comfort Zone. He will not endure a moment's discomfort from delayed gratification. He's a short-term hedonist who wants what he wants when he wants it, which is *now*. Long-term consequences be damned.

"The responsibilities of State vex Our Royal Person with boredom, mummy! We wish to play video games instead. Do make the servants fetch Us a bag of Cheetos and feed them daintily to Us lest Our royal fingers become cheesy whilst We play Our royal Xbox!"

THE INTOLERABLE LIE

The problem with discomfort isn't that it's uncomfortable, but that we so often act like it's *intolerable*. A good example is when people quit smoking. Have you noticed how it brings out the inner drama queen?

Imagined conversation:

Quitter: *"Oh my god, I would literally die for a cigarette right now!"*

Snarky Friend: *"Literally? Die? That sounds rather counterproductive."*

Quitter: *"I'm ready to snap. I want to rip everyone's heads off!"*

Snarky Friend: *"Well, that would be a tad extreme, don't you think? And messy."*

Quitter: *"You know, they say that nicotine is more addictive than heroin!"*

Snarky Friend: *"Yeah, I call BS on that one. I mean, it's not as if you're vomiting and having cold sweats. Quitting cigarettes is hard, but it's not that hard. You can do it.*

Quitter: *"How DARE you not support me?!"(Smashes vase against wall. Dramatically throws feathered boa over shoulder and stomps to the door.) "I'm so upset now that I simply have to smoke. I hope you're happy with yourself!"*

Snarky Friend: *"Wow. That went diva fast."*

The snarky but foolhardy friend is right. Nicotine's addictiveness is on par with caffeine. Take it away, and you feel a bit anxious and irritable, while intense cravings only last a few minutes. Yet we (I smoked for over twenty years) tell ourselves over and over again that quitting is insanely hard. So, when withdrawal symptoms hit, we are primed to interpret them as far worse than they really are. **We convince ourselves that mere temporary discomfort is intolerable when it is nothing of the sort.**

Think back to any goal you gave up on or habit you failed to break or build, and you'll often find that Resistance tricked you into believing your discomfort was intolerable. One tell-tale sign is when we use overwrought language to justify giving up:

This is just impossible! Everything I try always fails.

This is the worst thing that has ever happened—I give up!

It's like God hates me or something! Why even try?

Melodramatic frames like these are a kind of distorted reasoning.

Your goals may be challenging, but few are impossible.

You fail at some things, sometimes, but not all things all the time.

Far worse things have happened and, frankly, will happen than whatever challenge you are now facing.

And unless you are Pharaoh, and frogs are at this very moment raining down on your head, God is probably not conspiring against your success.

The more likely explanation for why we give up is that when we hit a rough patch of road or face a setback, it's **frustrating**.

Frustration is unpleasant.

So we naturally want to move away from it and towards what **is** pleasant: The Comfort Zone.

But since our goal is important, we need to justify our choice to give up (and thereby resolve cognitive dissonance). So we tell ourselves that the discomfort is far worse than it really is. That it is terrible, devastating, impossible, torturous, intolerable. When, really, it is none of these. It's just bad. It's just hard. It's just unpleasant. It just sucks.

I'm not saying that all this happens consciously; I'm just saying it happens.

All the time.

And we need to be on guard against it.

HOW TO EXPAND YOUR COMFORT ZONE

T.S. Eliot said, "Only those who risk going too far can possibly find out how far one can go." Taking that "risk," whether real or imagined, is the work of expanding our Comfort Zone. Here are some tools that will help you begin that challenging, but also exciting, work.

Reframe Discomfort

When you begin to feel discomfort while working on a goal, reframe the way you think about it.

Back to the quitting smoking example, you can think of withdrawal symptoms as withdrawal symptoms, or you can think of them as *healing* symptoms. The physical feelings of withdrawal are unchanged, but your experience of them changes significantly.

Tolerance for discomfort increased.

Comfort Zone expanded.

The same goes for major setbacks to your goals. When an external obstacle or your own self-sabotage knocks you down, it's natural to want to retreat from the pain of feeling like a failure or a fool or both. But this is precisely the time to unleash your inner Nietzsche and remind yourself that pain can be a refining fire and, *Was mich nicht umbringt, macht mich stärker.* "What does not kill me makes me stronger." Just as addictive withdrawals are symptoms of healing, the pain of failure is a symptom of being tempered for success.

Leverage Pain

One way to overcome the temptation to procrastinate or give up on goals is to imagine the more intense future pain you'll experience if you fail to achieve them. This turns negative and even catastrophic thinking to your advantage, making it a kind of leverage to pry you out of your Comfort Zone.

Going out drinking tonight instead of staying home and being a good boy sounds nice, but remember that last hangover I had? No way. I'm too old for that crap.

Eating carrots when I want to eat carrot cake kinda sucks. But if I don't stick to healthy eating habits, I'll probably end up on My 600lb Life in a few years. That would suck way more.

The idea of going to a therapist makes me feel weak and weird. But if I don't, I'll probably end up one of those homeless people who scream at the sky, or addicted to drugs to numb my pain, or both. Way worse. So, therapy it is.

Leveraging pain in this way works well for some people because it brings out their **fight** instinct. But for others, it may bring out the **flight** instinct. So if you find that imagining future pain from failure makes you want to retreat further into your Comfort Zone, then it's not the right tool for you.

A good test is to ask yourself how you respond to pressing deadlines. If you excel when the pressure is on, then leveraging pain in this way will probably work well for you. If you don't, it won't.

Leverage Pleasure

We can also expand our Comfort Zone by anticipating greater pleasure outside of it than the pleasure we experience within it.

Yes, binge-watching Netflix would be nice. But imagine how fantastic I'll feel after writing for three hours instead?

It would be nice to buy that awesome pair of black sandlot PF Fliers sneakers, but it will feel even better to reach my savings goal this month.

Telling naysayers off would feel pretty good. But showing them up, that would feel even better.

Buying crap, nice. Achieving financial freedom, priceless.

Nothing tastes as good as lean and healthy feels.

Unlike leveraging pain, leveraging pleasure works for everyone. Though to varying degrees. You can also use it in conjunction with leveraging pain by following this basic formula:

If I **don't do X**, the **pain of Y** will be terrible!
But if I **do X**, the **pleasure of Z** will be amazing!

As in: If I don't finish this chapter today, the pain of falling behind schedule will suck. But if I do finish this chapter today, I'll feel like a champ.

Exercise: Embrace Embarrassment

One reason we stay in our Comfort Zone is that we fear the judgement of others and embarrassment if we fail. But remember what Maude said to Harold in *Harold & Maude*: "Everyone has the right to make an ass out themselves. You can't let the world judge you too much."

Try this crazy thing: Inoculate yourself against embarrassment by making an ass out of yourself *intentionally*. Clown it up in public. Be silly. Do something nutty. Invite the scrutinizing gaze of strangers and you'll find that—

while you may get some judgey looks—it doesn't matter one damn bit.

Their judgment can't hurt you.

And far more people will smile at your antics, anyway.

Most people are afraid of embarrassment, so they admire and even envy those who are enjoying life and seem to give zero fucks about what others think. (So long as you're making an ass out of yourself and not being an obnoxious ass to others, that is.)

The fact is that **people are going to judge you no matter what you do, so you might as well be judged while having fun and living your life on your own terms.**

So make an ass out of yourself. Build up immunity to the real or imagined judgement of others. Do this, and fear of embarrassment will lose its power to keep you in the Comfort Zone.

Exercise: The Cold Shower Switch

Here's a practical little exercise to expand your Comfort Zone and simultaneously increase your Willpower. I've been doing this for over a year now, and am addicted.

At the end of your nice hot shower, quickly switch it to a cold shower. Start with a count to five and then, over the next few days or weeks, increase it to thirty seconds or a minute.

That's it.

I know it may sound silly, but there's evidence suggesting that the mild shock this causes your body can have all kinds of outsized benefits: It strengthens your cardiovascular system, improves your skin, and helps with both anxiety and depression. And, of course, it expands your

Comfort Zone, with a measurable increase in your Will-power.

Apply what we learned about framing here by thinking or speaking words that affirm the experience as positive rather than negative. Condition yourself to think of it as an invigorating challenge you are undertaking rather than an unpleasant hardship you are enduring.

You will feel all-powerful after doing this. "Behold! I have defeated cold water! I am unstoppable!" Try it and see for yourself.

LEAN INTO IT

You don't need to violently crash through the walls of your Comfort Zone like some goal berserker, success banshee, or the Kool-Aid Man. You just need to lean into discomfort, bit by bit, thereby stretching and gradually expanding your Comfort Zone.

Day by day to . . .

Walk a little further.
Work a little harder.
Stay a little later.
Save a little more.
Spend a little less.
Eat a little better.
Be a little braver.
Be a little kinder.
Delay gratification a little longer.

I already said that when you lean into discomfort, your Comfort Zone expands. This is reason enough to make a habit of challenging yourself, because the larger your Comfort Zone is, the more things you'll end up being able to accomplish with ease.

But the advantages of gradually expanding your Comfort Zone go much further. As you expand your Comfort Zone ...

You grow in Willpower.
You grow in Self-confidence.
You grow in character.
You grow in Self-respect.
You grow in resilience.
You grow in vision and ambition.
You grow in creativity.
You grow in all-around strength.

Marcus Aurelius said, "The impediment to action advances the action. What stands in the way becomes the way."

That's the truth about the Comfort Zone. **The point where you start to feel uncomfortable is precisely where you should look for opportunity and for growth.**

So feel out the walls of your Comfort Zone, and push. Keep pushing. Do this, and your Comfort Zone will expand. What stood in the way will become the way.

CHAPTER 20

Feel The Fear And Do It Anyway

Fear is the mind-killer. Fear is the little-death that brings total oblit-eration. I will face my fear. I will permit it to pass over me and through me. And when it has gone past I will turn the inner eye to see its path. Where the fear has gone there will be nothing. Only I will remain.

—FRANK HERBERT, DUNE

WE HAVE ALL EXPERIENCED those nightmares of being chased by a monster or something else dark and terrifying.

Often, we don't see what it is—We just sense a malevolent presence stalking us. We run and try to hide, but to no avail. Eventually, it corners us. At the very moment we know it's about to strike from the shadows, we wake up in a cold sweat.

I once read a book on lucid dreaming that said you must never run from these dark manifestations in your psyche, or they will continue to haunt your dreams. Instead, you must turn around and face them. When you do, promised the author, you will always find that they have no power. The only power they ever had was your fear and your flight. Face the beast and it will vanish, never to haunt you again.

I have yet to test this in the world of dreams (I'm not yet a lucid dreamer. It's on my *Dreamlist*). But I think we can all recognize that this is often true in the waking world. We know in our gut that if we could just muster the courage to face many of our fears, we'd probably find they are mere paper dragons.

But it's that *probably* we get hung up on.

I can be told, and rationally believe, that there is a 99.9999% chance I won't die in an airplane crash. But fear is rarely rational, so that 0.0001% chance of dying keeps me running from the airplane monster. I know, though, that the day is coming when I'm going to want to travel more. To do that, I'm going to need to turn around, face the fear, get on a plane and keep getting on planes until my aerophobia is defanged.

The same holds for many—probably most—of our worries.

Instead of ignoring the debt collection calls, we just need to pick up the phone, call a credit counseling service, and find out our options.

Instead of swimming away from relationship woes in an ocean of whiskey, we just need to have the talk we've both been avoiding.

Instead of constantly worrying about the future, we just need to sit our ass down and start planning for it.

Every time we turn around and face a specific fear, three important things happen:

One. Our self-confidence increases as we prove to ourselves that we have more courage and resilience than we previously imagined.

Two. Our world-confidence increases as we start to realize that most of our suffering is self-created, the result of making doom mountains out of uncertainty molehills. Life isn't out to get us. It's pretty benign. We are swaddled in benevolence and surrounded with blessings.

Three. Our threshold for worry increases as we begin to see that most of the things we had been worrying about weren't worth worrying about at all. It takes a lot more to ruffle our feathers after that.

As Abraham Maslow said:

One can choose to go back toward safety or forward toward growth. Growth must be chosen again and again; fear must be overcome again and again.

The bad news is that if we acquiesce to fear, we will not grow, and our days will become a series of retreats from life. The good news is that the more often we face our fears, the fewer fears there are to face. We become braver, bolder, more confident. Our days become a procession of victories.

SOME WAYS TO WORK THROUGH FEAR

Ask yourself if any worries that have been chasing you lately. Stop running.
Turn around.
Face them.

Or at least begin the process of facing them. I'm a cowardly lion and have probably had more fears and anxieties than most. I'm still working on some (Fear of flying, fear of spiders, fear of death). Others, thankfully, I've largely or entirely conquered (fear of crowds, fear of failure, fear of embarrassment). Here are some tools I've used in the fight that you may find helpful, too.

Sit With Your Fear

Our instinct is to flee when fear arises. But we need to realize that what we're usually running from isn't the thing we fear or even the fear itself. **It's the discomfort over feeling anxious, fearful or uncertain**. It's much like the discomfort avoidance we talked about in the last chapter, only more acute.

An antidote: Allow yourself to feel the discomfort rather than trying to avoid it. When you feel anxious or fearful about a goal, close your eyes and take a few deep breaths. Mentally observe the feeling of fear. Don't judge it, just notice it.

Sit with it for a spell.

This alone is usually sufficient to begin dissipating the fear.

Unpleasant feelings like fear are like unruly children who just want to get your attention for the sake of getting your attention. If you ignore them, they only get louder and more insistent. But if you take a moment to acknowledge them, they tend to calm down. Not always, but often.

Reframe Your Fear

Fear tells you you're working outside of your Comfort Zone, and as we talked about in the last chapter, that's where victory lives. Fear dissipates when you reframe it as a signpost of growth. So when fearful, reframe it:

My fear is proof positive that I'm precisely where I should be.

Or ...

My fear tells me that I'm on the right track.

Or ...

Overcoming this fear is just the challenge I need to take me to the next level.

Here's another way to think about reframing fear. Physiologically, anxiety and excitement are basically indistinguishable. They are both characterized by nervous energy, racing heart, butterflies in the stomach, a strange sense of disassociation from the world.

Think of getting on a rollercoaster. For some, it's exhilarating, for others terrifying, and still others a mix of both. The feelings in each case are the same. Only the interpretation of them differs. The framing.

Remember this when feeling anxious about a goal.

Try to interpret the feelings as excitement rather than anxiety. Change your physical state to reflect the reframe, too. Unknit your brow, straighten your back, smile large. "I get to ride a goalercoaster! Wooo hoo!"

(I should SO trademark "goalercoaster.")

Refuse To Catastrophize

There's an old saying often attributed to Mark Twain that goes, "I'm an old man and have known a great many troubles, but most of them never happened."

That's how Resistance uses fear to keep us in the Comfort Zone; it tells us all that can go wrong if we leave it. Our imaginations don't paint mere dreary landscapes of grey discomfort; they paint apocalyptic doomscapes with black and blood-red skies.

If you try stand-up at open mic night, they won't just *not* laugh. They'll boo, throw beer bottles at your face, and insult your parentage.

If you quit your safe but boring job to start an exciting home business, you won't merely fail. You'll end up in massive debt, definitely bankrupt, and probably homeless.

If you go on the date with the hot guy, you won't just feel awkward and tongue-tied. You'll also end up having uncontrollable blow-out diarrhea right there at the dinner table, and he'll tell everyone on social media, and then you'll be known as "Diarrhea Girl," and you'll have to leave town, but because of social media you can't escape the label, and you'll end up dying alone and then eaten by your seventy cats. So why even bother going on this stupid date in the first place?

You get the picture. We catastrophize normal anxiety into absurd fears, and the bigger the goal the more catastrophically we catastrophize.

When you catch yourself doing this, the fix is simple: **Don't**. Refuse to indulge the horror stories Resistance wants to tell. Remind yourself that catastrophic thinking is irrational—it's wacky screwball speculation lacking any supporting evidence.

If you catch yourself mid-horror-story, stop and notice the absurdity of it. Laugh at it, at Resistance, and at yourself. "What silly monkeys we can be, what with our scary stories!"

Argue With Your Fear

Our fears are rarely rational, so another good way to defeat them is to argue with them. When fear starts spinning tales of all that could go wrong or why you shouldn't pursue or continue with a goal, muster your best counter-arguments. You'll probably find that it won't take much since fear's arguments are so often over-the-top crazy, like Diarrhea Girl taught us.

So when Resistance starts to catastrophize, challenge it at every point. Pull the breaks and interrogate yourself with questions like:

- *Really now, is this scenario at all probable?*

- *What's irrational and downright crazy about this scenario?* (Look for the humor in it. Laugh at yourself.)

- *What is a more reasonable **worst**-case scenario? Couldn't I survive that?*

- *In fact, haven't I faced equal or bigger fails in the past, and come out just fine?* (Review your Victory List for examples.)

- *And what is a possible **best**-case scenario?*

Arguing rationally with those doomsday narratives, quickly unmasks their absurdity. Your fear will then be replaced by laughter, and courage.

Visualize Successful Outcomes

Visualize yourself boldly, bravely busting through your fears and coming out on the other side, having successfully achieved your goal.

When visualizing in this way, focus on feelings: First feeling the fear, then the feeling of bravely choosing to face the fear, and finally the feeling of triumph after you've passed through the fear.

Repeat this exercise daily until you've defeated the fear and pushed through to success, just as you visualized.

Try The Emotional Freedom Technique

The Emotional Freedom Technique (EFT), also called "Tapping Therapy," entails tapping your fingers at specific meridian points on your body while repeating phrases related to the fear. Why or how EFT works is up for debate, but I used it to effectively dissipate feelings of fear during an anxious period of my life.

Tapping is easy, and you can find plenty of videos on YouTube that will show you how to do it. Different practitioners may vary the tapping order or use somewhat different phraseologies, but don't get hung up on that. They are superficial differences and don't seem to impact the effectiveness of the EFT.

Use The Sedona Method

In June of 2020, I had my first anxiety attack in over twenty years. They continued for about two weeks. It was hell. I beat them back using *The Sedona Method*.

This is *The Sedona Method*, in a nutshell:

Step 1: Focus on the fear or negative feeling. Let yourself feel it for a moment.

Step 2: Ask yourself, "Could I allow myself to welcome this fear/anxiety?" Answer Yes or No.

Step 3: Ask yourself, "Could I let this feeling [or name the feeling] go?" Answer Yes or No.

Step 4: Ask, "Would I?" Answer Yes or No.

Step 5: Ask, "When?" Answer in whatever way feels right at that moment. "Now," "Never," Tomorrow," "Later," "I don't know," whatever.

Step 6: Repeat steps one through five until the fear or anxiety dissipates.

When the step calls for a yes or no answer, only give a yes or no answer. Then move to the next step. Don't get hung up on any step. Just be as clear and honest, focused, and concise as possible, and keep moving through them as many times as it takes for the fear or anxiety to dissipate.

Never Surrender

Make this one of your mantras: "I feel the fear but do it anyway." Covenant with yourself to no longer flee from fear, but to turn and face it, and to defeat it. No matter what it takes. Be dramatic and think of yourself as a warrior, fighting to realize your destiny, God's very own champion on a crusade for Success. **Know that your victory is assured.**

If you have more acute and specific fears, phobias, or anxieties holding you back, refuse to accept them as permanent. They are uninvited squatters in your life and will soon be evicted. While you may not know how to evict them right now, make it a goal to eventually do just that. Research, read, and seek professional support if necessary.

* * *

Facing fear may not be easy. In fact, it rarely is. But you can begin by noticing your fear when it shows up and then remind yourself that it only has power if you give it power.

Fear can't stop you.

You *can* feel the fear and do it anyway.

And the more you do, the less frightful fear becomes.

CHAPTER 21

Declutter Your Life

For nothing matters except life; and, of course, order.
— VIRGINIA WOOLF

GOALS DEMAND FOCUS. Focus hates distraction. Distraction springs from clutter. So if you want to succeed at your goals, clear out some of the clutter in your life. Organize and simplify in these four areas: Your *environment*, your *inputs*, your *relationships*, and your *responsibilities*.

YOUR ENVIRONMENT

A messy desk is rarely just a messy desk. It's often a symptom of messy headspace. If not that, it's a prescription for one. As goal achievers, we need to be clear-headed. So shred the old paperwork, discard the dried-up pens, straighten the pencils, label the file folders, and put everything in its proper place.

When you clear space in your life to work on your goals, you'll find that you'll have an easier time focusing on those goals. Clarity is tidy.

Exercise: Tidy Up Your Space

If your house or apartment is a mess, give it a good Spring cleaning and organizing. You can start by creating a smaller sanctuary of tidiness and order—in your bedroom, your home office, or your kitchen table—where you can focus with fewer distractions. This is where you will sit down every day to plan your goals and review your progress. Commit to keeping this space clean and organized from now on.

Next, begin to expand this zone of order over time until your entire house or apartment is tidy and organized. Create rules and systems to assure that it's kept that way (You'll learn how in the next chapter).

YOUR INPUTS

Earl Nightingale said, "We become what we think about most of the time." This is why, as Jim Rohn warned, you must "stand guard at the door of your mind."

If you permit negativity to have regular and unchecked access to your mind, it will inevitably manifest in your attitudes, behavior and life. Garbage in, garbage out.

Some of the worst mental inputs come from social media and what now passes for the "news." We all recognize that much of social media has become a cesspool of contention and a breeding ground for anxiety and rage. Gone are the sylvan days of people sharing pics of their morning bagel or trading funny kitten memes. Now it seems a gluttonous bacchanal of outrage or fear, depending on what the news, or politicians on the news, tell us to fear or hate on any given day.

Yes, we become what we think about most of the time. And if we consume chaos, we will think chaos, and our lives will join the chaos. That's no recipe for success or happiness.

We need to take charge of our inputs and become more discriminating about what information we consume. Here are some places to start.

Retrain The Algorithms

Refuse to respond to negative social media posts or click on negative news articles. Instead, only click on positive and uplifting inputs. Teach the predictive algorithms that you have new information tastes, and fewer negative posts or agitprop will appear in your feeds. They probably won't vanish entirely, because Big Tech wants to homogenize thought. But it's a start. And it helps.

Unfollow Negative People

I've known some fun, funny, loving, kind people whose online personas have—over the last few years—become hysterical, humorless, intolerant, and mean.

Maybe you have experienced this sad phenomenon too. If so, you may want to do what I have chosen to do and unfollow such people. That may seem harsh, but it comes down to this question: "Does this online connection add more than it takes from my joy and peace of mind?"

Unfollowing someone online doesn't mean you have to sever ties with them in real life. And with Facebook, at least, you can "unfollow" to stop seeing their posts without having to unfriend them.

For other social media platforms where an unfollow is obvious and you don't want to upset the person, consider a tactful blanket explanation that doesn't make them feel singled out. You might explain, for example, that you're going on a strict social media diet, but still want to be able to keep in touch with special people like them via email or text. Assuming that's true, of course.

Choose New Online Communities

Leave all the online groups and forums that clutter your feed and mind with negative posts. Join groups that add value rather than steal joy from your life.

I recently joined several drawing related groups on Facebook, and that one little change dramatically improved my social media experience. Suddenly my feed is sprinkled with inspiring drawings from people sharing inspiring art instead of yelling politics at each other. I'd almost forgotten what that was like.

Note: I created a new goal community website that you're welcome to join (See *Resources 2*).

Go On A News And Social Media Fast

If you're a news junkie, the best thing you can do for your mental health is to go on a news fast for one month. Don't worry; the world will keep spinning without you knowing everything that's wrong with it. And chaos factory talking heads will have plenty of new terrifying stories to entertain you with once you return.

If, that is, you even want to return.

Because you might just find that life gets better in inverse proportion to how much news you consume.

The same goes for social media. Pick a month to live entirely social media free, and stick with that commitment. This is guaranteed to refresh your mind and spirit, especially if you take your news and social media fasts at the same time.

Choose More Positive Inputs

Use some of the time you've saved by eliminating negative information inputs to consume more positive things. Read some books or blog posts about goals, success, health, or financial freedom. Sign up for an art class. Meditate more. Go for a walk. Decluttering your mind and life is about making space for something better.

YOUR RELATIONSHIPS

Drama is messy. If there are people in your life who always pull you into their drama, it may be time to exit stage right. Or at least set some healthy boundaries.

The same goes for those who want to suck you into their woe is me stories, their I'm a victim stories, or their self-righteous rage stories (⇐This last one was *SO* me).

It's one thing to support those you care about, quite another to enable them, and quite another still to enable them at the expense of your own sanity. Being genuinely supportive of others often begins by being a bit selfish and learning to first support ourselves. As Ayn Rand said, "To say, 'I love you' one must first know how to say the 'I.'"

YOUR RESPONSIBILITIES

Are you always the first to volunteer for new projects? Are you a fixer that can't ignore a problem, even if it's not your own? Are you a helper who just can't seem to help yourself from always helping? If so, this is a noble trait. But as Hesiod wrote circa 700BC, "Observe due measure; moderation is best in all things." That includes good things, like being a helpful fixer who volunteers to helpfully fix things.

If our plates are too full, we need to learn portion control. If you have so many responsibilities that you can't find time to focus on your goals, then you have chosen to take on too many responsibilities. Resistance may be using that as an excuse for you to avoid taking responsibility for the most important thing of all: your own life outcomes.

It's like the soccer mom who says, "Well I'd love to write a romance novel, but I have to take all the kids to soccer practice, and then to ballet practice, and then host the glee club fundraiser bake sale, and then go to the PTA meeting. It's my responsibility as a parent!"

As a longtime fan of the classic show Roseanne, I imagine Roseanne responding to said soccer mom with something like:

Roseanne: *Bull crap. Our responsibility as parents is to love 'em, feed 'em and keep 'em from dying, while trying not to screw them up in the head too much. My kids turned out just fine without all that other stuff you're talking about.*

Darlene *(during her dark and mopey stage) slouches by.*

[Audience laughter]

Roseanne: *Well, two out of three ain't so bad.*

[More audience laughter]

Like the soccer mom, we sometimes imagine our responsibilities are absolute and inescapable, when they're nothing of the sort. Maybe she doesn't have to host the bake sale, or maybe she could skip the PTA meeting. She could simplify her life by being more selective in what responsibilities she decides to take on. And in the space created by this decluttering, she could find a bit of time each day to work on her romance novel.

This isn't to say she should choose the romance novel over soccer practice, by the way. It's only to say that she should get clear about her choices and her real options.

Exercise: Review Inputs, Relationships And Responsibilities

Review your inputs, relationships, and responsibilities in your goal journal, looking for unnecessary and burdensome complexity. Brainstorm ways you can begin to simplify in each area.

Questions to consider:

What steps will I take to reduce or eliminate the news?
Take them.

What steps will I take to reduce or eliminate exposure to negativity on social media?
Take them.

Are there other inputs that keep stealing my peace of mind, my joy, or otherwise distract me? How can I tidy up?
Do it.

What are some positive inputs I can replace those negative ones with?

Replace them.

Are there people who keep drawing me into drama or other negativity? Do I need to set some boundaries? What kind?

Set them.

Have I taken on too many responsibilities? Can I opt out, offload, delegate, or reduce them?

Do so.

Are there other areas of my life I can simplify? What? How?

Try it.

* * *

Decluttering your environment, inputs, relationships, and responsibilities simplifies your life and creates more of the physical, mental and emotional room you need to focus on your goals.

Next you'll discover another way to simplify and free up even more time for achieving your goals.

CHAPTER 22

Create Rules, Rituals, And Systems

Each problem that I solved became a rule which served afterwards to solve other problems.

— RENE DESCARTES

THREE MAGIC TECHNIQUES will skyrocket your effectiveness as a goal achiever by simplifying decision-making and automating much of your daily routine. They are: *Setting Rules, creating Rituals,* and *establishing Systems.*

RULES

I am by nature rebellious and distrustful of authority, so I tend to chafe against rules. One sometimes-exception is with rules that I create for myself, especially for habit goals.

Too often, we squander time and mental energy wrestling with ourselves over doing what we know we need to do. "I want to start the day early—But I'm so tired and want to sleep—But I promised myself I'd get up—But maybe I can snooze for just ten minutes—But ..."

Rules are a powerful antidote to this kind of all-too-human nonsense. When you have a rule in place, you no longer need to think about what to do. The rule automatically kicks in and decides for you.

Most rules follow the format of **If X then Y.** For example, the first rule I set for myself was "If Sunny, Then I walk." If I look out the window on any given day, and it is sunny, then I walk at least one mile at some point during the day. Period. No thinking about it, no arguing with myself. If X, then Y. If Sunny, Walk. It worked, too. I've maintained this rule since 2017 without (I think) breaking it even once.

Recovery Rules

You can also set recovery rules for when you slip up with a bad habit or find yourself indulging in unhealthy habitual mental patterns.

Examples:
- *If I have a Dr. Pepper, **then** I will walk another five hundred steps.*
- *If tempted to look at porn, **then** I will distract myself with exercise.*
- *If I start feeling the sads, **then** I will call a friend.*
- *If Monkey Mind starts raging against the machine, **then** I will take a slow, deep breath and exhale Om, Shanti, Shanti, Shanti.*

Create Rules, Rituals, And Systems

- *If I respond reactively to a political post on social media, **then** I will immediately delete my comment.*

Don't beat yourself up if at first you forget to activate the rule or aren't consistent with it. It takes time to make a rule habitual. Just keep working at it.

Exercise: Create Two Rules

Create one rule for a positive discipline or habit you want to instill and one recovery rule for a bad habit you are trying to break. Post the rules where you will see them daily, and practice activating them. Once one a rule becomes habitual, add a new one.

RITUALS

Rituals are a series of habits strung together. A rule may activate the first habit, which then triggers the second, which triggers the third until the entire ritual is complete. Like a line of falling dominoes.

In *Free To Focus*, Michael Hyatt advocates dividing your day by four rituals:

Morning Ritual

This begins as soon as you wake up and continues until you start work.

Example: Brewing morning coffee, showering, dressing, morning inspirational reading, daily planning, commute.

Work Startup Ritual

This consists of the first tasks you do every day when starting work.

201

Example: Turning on the computer, checking and responding to emails, reviewing work agenda.

Work Closedown Ritual

This consists of tasks to close out your workday.

Example: Shutting down the computer, sending final emails, checking messages, tidying up the desk.

Evening Ritual

This closes out your day.

Example: Evening review, evening reading, nightly prayer.

Hyatt's approach is great, but don't feel constrained by it. For example, my morning ritual *includes* some of my work, and that works for me:

1. Drink a large glass of water.
2. Brush teeth + splash face with cold water 3x.
3. Brew coffee.
4. Make bed.
5. Pour coffee.
6. Plan day.
7. Write for three hours.

Floating Rituals

If you are self-employed or otherwise have a flexible schedule, consider using what I call floating rituals. These are rituals that follow a set pattern but have no set time during the day.

So, for example, you could have a ritual consisting of spiritual reading, meditation, and success visualizations that you do every day, but not necessarily at the same time every day.

Exercise: Create A Daily Ritual

Create your first daily ritual. I recommend starting with just a morning ritual, practicing and refining it for a month or so, and only then adding more rituals to other parts of your day.

SYSTEMS

Systems are similar to rituals, but they are more about batching related tasks than creating strings of habits. They are usually work related, but not necessarily.

Examples:

✓ I have a Webmaster Checklist that I go through once a week that lists website maintenance tasks like updating plugins, reviewing comments, running a speed test, and so on.

✓ You could create a daily Inbox System that regulates how and when you process your inbox and respond to emails each day. You can then plug this into your morning or work rituals.

✓ You can have Recovery Systems based on *If-Then* rules, like a hangover recovery plan or a checklist of actions to take when your website crashes.

Exercise: Create A System

Choose a daily activity or series of activities to systematize. A good place to start is with your inbox. Instead of checking and responding to emails randomly throughout the day, assign specific times for processing and responding to messages.

In *Chapter 4*, you brainstormed possible workarounds to obstacles you might encounter when pursuing your goals. Refer back to that exercise now and see if you can create a recovery system for any of them.

It may help to use the *If-Then* approach as in, "If I encounter obstacle X, Then I will take the following emergency steps: Step A, Step B, Step C," and so on.

* * *

Aristotle said, "Freedom is obedience to self-made rules." I could do without the word "obedience," but the point is well taken. Rules, rituals, and systems sound uptight, constrictive, and creativity-stifling. But it's the exact opposite. By creating rules, rituals, and systems for relatively trivial activities, we free up more time to focus on what's important: Our goals and living a breakthrough life.

CHAPTER 23

Create A Vision Board

Create a vision of who you want to be, and then live into that picture as if it were already true.

— ARNOLD SCHWARZENEGGER

A VISION BOARD, also sometimes called a dream board, is essentially a cut and paste collage of images and words depicting your goals. In being image-rich, vision boards are a great way to communicate your desires to your subconscious mind. Your subconscious will, in turn, search for ways to make that vision a reality in your life. It's a wonderful and fun goal achievement tool.

CREATING YOUR VISION BOARD USING THE INTUITIVE METHOD

To create a vision board, set aside some time when you won't be disturbed and follow the steps below. I call this *The Intuitive Method* of creating a vision board.

Step 1. Collect Image-Rich Magazines

With your goals in mind, go on an image collecting adventure. You could do this online, but it's far more fun to go to a secondhand shops and collect a bunch of magazines.

Step 2. Collect Your Tools And Get In The Zone

Get an 8"x11" or 11"x17" piece of paper, construction paper, or poster board. You can also use one of the free templates provided in *Resources 1*.

Grab a pair of scissors and some glue (I prefer glue sticks).

Claim an hour or so of time when you won't be disturbed. Turn off your phone. Put on some relaxing music and center yourself with a few slow, deep breaths.

Constructing a vision board is a creative process that works best from a relaxed and *intuitive* headspace. Ergo, "The Intuitive Method."

Step 3. Build Your Image Pool

With your goals in mind, go through each magazine, one by one, and cut out any images that inspire or speak to you.

Don't worry about cutting out the images perfectly. You can do that later. If you're not sure about an image but think you may want to use it, go ahead and cut it out. For now, you're just creating a pool of images to choose from later.

Don't try to find the perfect images. After all, it's unlikely that you'll find the exact picture of your dream home interior, exterior, and all the furnishings. But you could find one or two that come close, plus a few pics of mid-century modern furniture that evoke the spirit and feel of your dream home.

Also cut out any headlines or words from headlines that jump out at you and relate to your goals. Put these in a separate pile.

Step 4. Choose And Add Images

Now the real fun begins! Set aside your magazines. Drawing from your pool of images, start piecing together your vision board.

Don't glue the images down willy nilly. Instead, move them around on the board, paying attention to how they look and feel in relation to each other.

This is an exercise in mindfulness and creative receptivity. Whether you are aware of it or not, you have an instinct for visual composition that will give you hints of where images work and don't work.

Similarly, trust your feelings here because these are cues from your subconscious.

That said, there's no right or wrong way to do this. Just go with the creative flow.

Once you have a feel of where the images belong, trim them down, and glue them in place.

I recommend aiming for an image-rich board that doesn't leave much white space. A large white field with a few lonely images just isn't inspiring. It should have enough images to keep your eye moving. A roving eye is a tell-tale sign that your creative, subconscious mind is delighted and engaged. And that's precisely what you want in a vision board.

Step 5. Add Inspiring Words

If there are any words or short sentences that you cut out and want to add, do that now. Be conservative with adding words. They should serve the images, not steal focus from them. Words that evoke a positive emotional response are best.

USING YOUR VISION BOARD

You now have an inspired and inspiring vision board! Post your vision board where you will see it every day. Try to spend a minute or two every morning and night looking at it. Allow the images to soak into your subconscious mind.

If you have a bit more time, let the vision board be a springboard for fantasy. Daydream about how wonderful it will be to be financially free, have massive confidence, turn heads, own that new home, or travel the world.

MORE VISION BOARD TIPS AND IDEAS

Go Digital

Like I said, I much prefer the tactile approach of cutting, pasting, and creating a tangible vision board, but I have made digital versions too.

If you prefer that route, search online for images and use Canva.com (It's free) to create your digital vision board. Size it for use as a desktop wallpaper so you'll see it whenever using the computer.

Take A Picture

Take a photo of your vision board and set it as the lock screen image on your phone.

Make Multiple Vision Boards

Instead of having one vision board for all of your goals, consider creating a vision board for each individual life domain: a *Health & Fitness* vision board, a *Wealth* vision board, a *Vocation* vision board, and so on.

Create A Vision Journal

This works the same way as a vision board while giving you and your vision room to grow over time. Fill your goal journal or loose pages in a three-ring binder with inspiring images and words that you collect over time.

- Collect any inspiring images you come across and add them to your ever-evolving vision journal.
- You can have one page for your main vision board and additional pages for specific domains or goals.
- Add inspiring quotes and new images as you find them.
- Fortune cookie fortunes go here, of course!
- Paste clippings from inspiring articles in the vision journal.
- Create mind-maps of your goals and dreams.
- Draw and doodle your dreams. The creative sky is the limit with your vision journal.

Draw Your Vision Board

As an alternative to the traditional collage style, try drawing or painting your vision board. Be courageous with color when doing so, and don't worry about making it perfect. The point is to enjoy the process while communicating your goals to your subconscious mind. And your subconscious mind is not concerned with realism. It's concerned with feeling. So, your vision board could have stick figures and look like it was drawn by a five-year-old, but if it evokes positive emotions, then it's a masterpiece.

* * *

I've noticed something funny about vision boards or, more accurately, how people think of them. Those who poo-poo them as a waste of time best suited to New Age hacks seem to waste more time and be far less successful than those vision board lovin' New Age hacks they like to criticize.

Far from being do-nothing dreamers with their heads in clouds, it's very often the folks with vision boards who are the real take-action achievers. Not always, but often enough that it convinced me to use (and enjoy) this tool.

Make one for yourself and see what happens. You may be surprised.

CHAPTER 24

Find Allies

When two or more people coordinate in a spirit of harmony they place themselves in position, through alliance, to absorb power directly from the great storehouse of Infinite Intelligence.

— NAPOLEON HILL

THE ENEMIES ARRAYED against our success are legion. There's Resistance, which fights to keep us safely stuck. Advertisers who want us insecure and needy for what they have to sell. Politicians and the so-called "news" media who want us slack-jawed, sheepish, and obedient. Stalinesque cancel culture commissars who want us so afraid of saying or doing the wrong thing we never say or do anything at all. Even some of our well-meaning friends and family may apply conscious or semi-conscious pressure on us to give up dreams that threaten their Comfort Zone.

To beat back all these anti-achievement Huns, we need allies. Other goal-oriented people who *get it*. Non-conformists and dreamers, like you. They don't have to have the same goals (though that works too). They just need to have goals and be committed to achieving them. Support from allies like these can save your life. The life of fabulous success that you are working to create.

Allies come in four basic types: *Goal Buddies*, *Mastermind Groups*, *Mentors*, and *Coaches*. Let's look at each.

GOAL BUDDIES

Goal buddies are friends who support each other in the pursuit of their goals. It's an alliance of equals, though just like any friendship, each of you may bring unique strengths to the table and be more or less successful in different areas of life. Here are some benefits of having goal buddies:

Accountability

When we share our goals with others we feel more accountable. We don't want to disappoint them or embarrass ourselves by failing. And this is powerful leverage. Regular meetings with a goal buddy habituate this leverage.

Perspective

When facing obstacles on the path of success we can get so wrapped up in the problem that we lose perspective. The solution may be right under our nose, but we just can't see it. That's when a goal buddy can prove invaluable. Your goals are not their goals. Since they are standing on the outside looking in, they may see something you can't. Or they may think of novel solutions you wouldn't have considered because you're too close to the problem.

Praise

We crave and deserve praise for a job well done or a goal well achieved. It reinforces our commitment to success and simply feels good. A good goal buddy will be generous in offering praise.

Encouragement

When unexpected setbacks happen—as they will—and nothing seems to be going according to plan, it's only natural to feel discouraged. A good goal buddy can and will support and encourage you at such times by reminding you of all the things you already know but just need to hear. Like, "You can do it. You got this. I believe in you!"

Enthusiasm

Enthusiasm can be contagious. On days you're feeling *blah*, the excitement your goal buddy has for her current project may rub off on you. And visa versa. It's a fabulous feedback loop of enthusiasm.

Healthy Competition

Don't underestimate the power of healthy competition to fuel your success. It's what created and sustains the miracle of modern Capitalism and every invention, innovation, and creature comfort it has given us. The threads of healthy (and sometimes unhealthy) competition also weave through much of History's greatest art and philosophy.

With a goal buddy, competition isn't about winning, per se, since you will rarely if ever have precisely the same goals. It's also rarely if ever an overt competition. Rather, it's that tamed and perfectly natural wee bit of envy that arises when you see the success of someone you care about. While truly and genuinely happy for them . . . A naughty competitive little part of you also wants to one-up them.

That naughty competitive little part of you is healthy. Let him or her play.

Choosing Your Goal Buddies

When choosing a goal buddy, pick someone you trust, who is committed to achieving goals, and who will stick to regular meetups or check-ins for the long haul.

As a rule, avoid picking a goal buddy whose life is in shambles or that you think will otherwise require a lot more support than they can give. This would be a mentoring relationship (with you as mentor) more than a goal buddy relationship. While mentoring is great, it's not the same as a goal buddy relationship, which is meant to be more of a two-way street.

I recommend meeting up with your goal buddy around the first of every month to share your plans, then touching bases every week or two for brief progress reports.

MASTERMIND GROUPS

You may want to have multiple goal buddies that you meet with individually or as a group. These are called *Mastermind Groups* or simply *Masterminds*.

Having a Mastermind is especially valuable when you have one or more goal buddies who are focused on the same life domains or have similar ambitions. For example, you might have a goal buddy to discuss *Health & Fitness* goals with, another to discuss your entrepreneurial goals with, and so on.

While you may meet with each goal buddy separately, in aggregate they become your Mastermind Group.

Alternately, your Mastermind Group could be a bunch of goal-oriented friends who meet up for coffee and casual goal-talk once a month or so. This approach, while less focused, can still be very rewarding.

MENTORS

Where goal buddies are an alliance of equals, mentors support you with their greater experience, insight, and wisdom.

A good mentor has already succeeded where you want to succeed and is open to sharing what they know. Most successful people are happy to do so when asked because most successful people have had mentors of their own and feel it's important to pay that forward.

You may want to find different mentors for different domains. A dirt-poor but brilliant novelist could make a fabulous writing mentor, but you'd be foolish to listen to his investment advice.

SUCCESS COACHES

Having a Life Coach or Success Coach is a great way to support your goals and buttress yourself against adversity on the path of achieving those goals. Many of the most successful success coaches still meet with their own success coaches, which says a lot about how successful success coaching can be. (That's a tongue twister!)

Unlike goal buddies and mentors, you'll have to pay for coaching. But goal achievers are willing to invest in themselves, and a great coach is worth the investment.

While there are certifying organizations for life and success coaching, quality varies. In any case, I don't think formal or semi-formal credentials matter much. After all, it's not some certificate from the Jedi Academy that makes a powerful Master Jedi. It's his skill in the Force. That's just science.

Look for testimonials, blog posts, or books they've published. Find out how long they've been coaching. Ask them about their method and their areas of coaching expertise. Do a bit of due diligence.

If after meeting with a coach you don't click, end the coaching relationship quickly and respectfully. Don't waste their time, or your time and money, on a coaching relationship that doesn't excite you.

* * *

I may need to find a writing coach to help me figure out a good way to conclude my chapters because it's my least favorite part of writing. It feels so forced sometimes, doesn't it? Like, "Now that you've learned X, let's turn to the next chapter where we'll talk about Y!"

Anyway, on an entirely unrelated note . . .

Now that you've learned about finding success allies, let's turn to the next chapter where we'll talk about being a possibility thinker!

CHAPTER 25

Be A Possibility Thinker

Success is a matter of luck. Just ask any failure.

— EARL WILSON

FAILURES ARE FATALISTS who, in their secret heart of hearts, are convinced that the universe is plotting against them, and there's not a hell of a lot they can do about it. "Why try when I'll probably fail?" is their profession of faith(lessness). And if they do try, the first obstacle they encounter is taken as a sure sign that they should give up. "I guess it's not meant to be," they sigh. Or, "I guess I don't have what it takes." They believe themselves the helpless victims of everything from circumstances to upbringing to social injustice to the alignment of the stars. When, in fact, they are victims of their own minds. Their lives are stuck because their thinking is fixed.

Successful people, on the other hand, say with Emerson, "You think me a child of my circumstances: I make my circumstances."

They say too with John F. Kennedy, "Things don't happen. Things are made to happen."

Successful people are usually some hue of optimist. They believe life is, at worst, a benign field of opportunity and that they need to make the most of it. At best, it's positively benevolent and conspiring for their benefit. And they need to make the most of that, too.

When it comes to hardships, successful people aren't Pollyanna's who are blind to life's storms, mind you. They just know that every storm will pass and that it's their job to steer the best course they can through or around it. "I'll figure it out" is their motto. "I got this!" is their credo. Where failures see only limitation, they see possibility.

Possibility-oriented thinkers are like the story of the boy who was asked if he could play the piano. "I don't know," he answered. I've never tried."

Or like the story of another boy who was drawing a picture:

"What are you drawing?" the teacher asked.

"God," the boy answered.

"But no one knows what God looks like," said the teacher.

"Well, I'm not done yet!" said the boy.

If we want to be successful, we need to grow in possibility-oriented thinking. Here are some mindset-shifting tools that will help.

ACT AS IF

When you are sure of the goal but doubt your capacity to achieve it, take a big breath, close your eyes, say a little prayer, and leap. Remember the words of Goethe:

What you can do, or dream you can, begin it, Boldness has genius, power, and magic in it. Only engage, and then the mind grows heated; Begin it, and the work will be completed!

Don't forever hem and haw and hedge your bets around important goals.

Go all in.

Act as if it's impossible to fail.

When you're afraid, act as if you have faith. When you're confused, pretend you know what the hell you're doing, no problem, easy peasy lemon squeezy!

Just remember that acting as if you can't fail assumes that you first *act*. Sometimes that means rolling the dice. As Teddy Roosevelt said, "In any moment of decision, the best thing you can do is the right thing. The worst thing you can do is nothing."

So do something, confident that even if it's not the right thing, it will bring you one step closer to finding it.

ASK "HOW CAN I?"

I was watching an interview with Robert Kiyosaki, author of *Rich Dad Poor Dad*, where he says that one of the biggest differences between the mindsets of poor people and rich people, is that when confronted with challenges rich people don't say, "I can't." They ask, "How can I?"

This was a mind-shifter for me.

Especially when it comes to our biggest, most attractive, and most ambitious goals, we can become so intimidated by the magnitude of the task before us that we begin to lose faith and second-guess ourselves before we've even started.

"I can't." We think it. We feel it.

At such times merely affirming "Yes I can!'" may not be enough.

We need to convince ourselves.

Asking, "How can I?" does just that.

Can't, closes doors. It's final. There is no court of appeals after *Can't.*

How Can I? not only leaves the doors open, it looks for unlocked windows and tips books on the shelf, looking for a hidden lever to a secret door.

I'll never get out of debt!
How can I *get out of debt?*

I can't stick to a diet to save my life!
How can I *lose weight in a healthy and sustainable way?*

I hate working out.
How can I *enjoy exercising?*

I'll always be alone.
How can I *be happy alone?*
And/or **How can I** *put myself where my soulmate can find me?*

I could never start my own business.
How can I *be self-employed?*

I can't even draw a stick figure.
How can I *improve my drawing?*

I have an anxiety disorder.
How can I *become permanently free of anxiety?*

Don't shoot yourself in the foot before even trying to run the race. (Or after you've run the race, for that matter.) If you have a goal and Resistance says, "I can't," refuse to accept that as the final verdict. Challenge your self-limiting thinking by asking, "How can I?"

EMBRACE BEGINNERS MIND

In the beginner's mind there are many possibilities, but in the expert's there are few.

— SHUNRYU SUZUKI

When I was about twelve and learning to draw, my pencil often stubbornly refused to accurately depict whatever it was I was looking at. While I was otherwise a fairly gentle and sensitive boy, at those moments I'd transform into a raging art diva. I'd curse and tear the drawing into tiny pieces. I'd break my pencil in half and throw the pieces across the room.

I'm sure that part of that was puberty, which is well known to release excessive diva hormones. But it wasn't just that. I know it wasn't, because now, in my late forties, I'm learning how to draw with pen and ink. And while I haven't yet thrown a fit and torn up any drawings, I've sure as hell been tempted to. The depletion of diva hormones that comes with aging has surely helped keep me from having tantrums. Taking slow, deep breaths, too. And one more thing, apropos to this section: I remind myself to approach drawing with a beginner's mind.

This is useful for many goals, especially those for building a new habit or developing a new skill. We think our frustration comes from how hard the new habit or skill is to learn. That's not usually the real problem. The real problem—and source of our self-created frustration—is that we want to leap from student to master and skip over all the messy parts in between.

At twelve, I'm looking at a drawing of Spider Man created by an artist who had been drawing comics for years, and it's awesome. I want my copy of it to be just as awesome, but it's not. Mine sucks Spidey balls.

Same thing at forty-eight: I see brilliant, inspiring, intimidating ink drawings on Instagram, and I want to be that good too. I draw unskillfully while thinking I should draw skillfully, even though I haven't yet developed the skill. This is wrong thinking.

Right thinking is beginner's mind. Beginner's mind is approaching the goal or skill you're trying to learn with the receptive, playful, but also serious spirit of a child. Look at five year old kid, drawing a picture with crayons. Intense but loose focus, slow and careful lines here, reckless and wild scribbles there, dubious but brave color choices, and . . . Why is mommy riding a flying pink turtle and breathing lightening while holding a sword in one hand and fifth of Jack Daniels in the other? Who knows. But it's brilliant, and it's going on the fridge.

Engaging goals with a beginner's mind frees you to be experimental and inventive, which are both essential ingredients to success in life. Fear of imperfection or failure no longer holds you back because you don't expect perfection.

Yes, you still crave mastery, and you trust it will come. In *time*. For now, you're content to be the student who is learning. And it's precisely through this open, flexible, and playful mindset of the beginner that you will more rapidly progress to your goal of mastery.

LOOK FOR A BETTER WAY

Do the best you can until you know better. Then when you know better, do better.

— MAYA ANGELOU

This, too, is beginner's mind: Don't immediately settle for the obvious route to achieve your goals. Ask yourself if there might be a better way.

Can I accomplish the same or similar goal with less effort?

Am I making this unnecessarily complicated?

How can I streamline this to get it done faster?

Is this step necessary to achieve my goal, or have I just convinced myself it's necessary?

Has anyone achieved this goal faster/easier than common wisdom says is possible? How?

Is there a different way?

Is there an easier way?

Is there a more enjoyable way?

Is there a better way?

Asking questions like these can produce novel and inspired ideas for achieving your goals with less effort and in less time.

Never uncritically accept what conventional wisdom says about how you should live your life, either. Conventional wisdom rarely creates extraordinary lives. Plus, it's quite often dead wrong.

TAKE AN INFORMED LEAP OF FAITH

Of course, going to the opposite extreme is a bad idea too. Worse than failing to ask questions in search of a better approach to achieving your goals, is asking so many questions that you fail to take any action at all. Paralysis by analysis is real, and it's a success killer.

As David Schwartz said, "We must be willing to make an intelligent compromise with perfection lest we wait forever before taking action."

And as Teddy Roosevelt said, "Do what you can, with what you have, where you are."

Strike a balance between inquiry and action by asking questions and getting the best answers you can. Armed with this knowledge, take action using your best judgement. Don't wait or forever search for the perfect plan, because there is no such animal. Take an informed leap of faith.

* * *

Turn your back on the suffocating thinking of fatalists who believe that life is a zero-sum game. Instead, approach your goals and life with an open spirit and a mindset oriented towards what is possible.

When you do this, you'll find that Napoleon Hill was right: "Whatever the mind can conceive and believe, it can achieve."

If it's possible, it's possible for *you*.

CHAPTER 26

Not Sure? Prototype

Absorb what is useful, discard what is not, add what is uniquely your own.

— BRUCE LEE

WHAT IF YOU AREN'T SURE what you want to do with your life, or what your most important goals should be?

Answer: Prototype.

YOUR LIFE AS A SUPERWIDGET

Imagine the intrepid inventor who wants to create the next big thing, the SuperWidget. While he has a few vague ideas, he's not really sure what the SuperWidget even does. It needs to be super—That much at least is certain. And it should be widgety, or at the very least widgetesque.

Beyond that, he's willing to experiment.

And that's what he does. He drafts a design, builds his first prototype, readies the first test. He flips the switch.

With a beautiful hum, SW Prototype 1 glows to life. But the inventor's excitement is short lived because only seconds later SW Prototype 1 sparks, sputters, and dies in a cloud of smoke.

The inventor sighs, disappointed.

But he knew getting it perfect on the first go was unlikely. "Back to the drawing board," he says.

He evaluates the results of his first experiment. He thinks about what went wrong and how he might get it right. This actually inspires an idea for another feature. He tweaks his design and then creates SW Prototype 2.

This version stays alive a little longer, has fewer sparks, and though it too fails, there is no cloud of smoke.

Good sign.

Back the drawing board.

Evaluate again. Tweak the design. New prototype. New test. Back to the drawing board. Evaluate again. Tweak the design. New prototype. New test. Sputter. Sparks. Stop.

And so it goes until, at last, it happens. No sputters. No sparks. No stop. Just the sweet, steady hum of success. "By the gods!" He shouts in triumph. "This is the most widgety of widgets that has ever widgeted! And nothing wrought by man has ever been more super!" Soon, SW Prototype 8 will hit the shelves as SuperWidget Model 1.0, the next big thing.

That's what you do in life when you're not sure what to do in life. You pick a big goal, and you experiment with it. You don't have to be sure it's what you want. It just has to be something you think you might like.

You draft a plan.

You try it out (Or at least some *version* of it).

You may find you need to tweak the goal. Or you may discover that the goal isn't right for you at all. In either case, you return to the drawing board to modify and refine or start from scratch.

You then set a new goal.

Wash, rinse, and repeat.

Do this enough times and you'll discover inspiring goals and prototype your way into a breakthrough life.

CHOOSING WHAT TO PROTOTYPE

If you're still not sure what goals to start prototyping, here are four steps that will help you decide. They're my own riff on steps outlined in *Designing Your Life* by Bill Burnett and Dave Evans.

Step1: Brainstorm Possibilities

Create a list of goal ideas. Refer to your *Dreamlist* and the ideal life envisioning exercises you did in *Part 2*. Ponder possible goals, feel out your desires, play make-believe. Brainstorm. Write down every idea. Don't pause to evaluate their practicality or relevance. That comes next.

Step 2: Winnow

Too many options can paralyze us with indecision, so you need to narrow down your list. Start with a gut-check, looking for any goals that **don't** really speak to you. Strike them off the list. Then do a gut check for any goals that **do** speak to you. Put a star next to them.

Next, do some research. Look into what it may take to achieve each goal. Brainstorm possible alternative routes to achieving the same goal.

Continue this winnowing dialogue between gut and brain, feeling and reason, until you've narrowed your selection down to your top three to five options.

Step 3: Choose Wisely

The thoughtful and heartful deliberation in Step 2 assures that your final choice will be a wise one because wisdom here isn't about being a prophet who foresees the future and knows what course of action to take. **Wisdom is simply making the best choice you can, where you are, with what you know**.

That's it.

Make your choice, trusting that your mind and heart have guided you well.

Step 4: Let Go And Try

Once you've made your wise choice, Resistance will tempt you to look back, second-guess, and reconsider.

Don't.

It can feel scary to commit to a course of action, but we can temper that fear by reminding ourselves that this is, after all, only prototyping. You're trying the goal on for size. If it doesn't fit, you can always try on another later.

PROTOTYPING TIPS

Here are some more prototyping tips to ponder.

Give It Sufficient Time

As I mentioned, I'm currently teaching myself to draw in pen and ink, which is a creative stretch goal for me since ink is unforgiving and intimidating.

I did a drawing the other day that was so terrible that I wanted to give up and go back to a medium I'm comfortable with (pencil). But I reminded myself that it's not pen and ink I'm frustrated with, it's the learning curve. In fact, I can't even be sure of whether or not I'll enjoy this medium until I push past the first steep incline of being terrible at it. I have to become at least *moderately* comfortable with it before deciding if it's right for me. Beginner's mind, remember?

Moral of the story: Give yourself time enough to get to know the goal you're prototyping, and not just the early and difficult learning curve of that goal.

Build On What Works

When a goal you're prototyping isn't quite working, and you need to go back to the drawing board, that doesn't always mean starting over from scratch. Ask yourself what part of the goal is working and see if you can build from that. Eliminate only what isn't working.

Enjoy The Process

Think of prototyping as play. Unlike with most goals where we know our target outcome, a prototype goal is open-ended. We benefit from approaching it with a playful and experimental spirit.

Read Designing Your Life

Designing Your Life: How To Build A Well-Lived, Joyful Life by Bill Burnett & Dave Evans is the definitive book on life prototyping.

* * *

Don't wait around for the clouds to part and angels to trumpet your grand life purpose—Seek it out for yourself through prototyping. In a sense, that is the purpose of life. To experiment, explore, play, and grow. Prototyping is just doing all that in a deliberate and directed way.

CHAPTER 27

4 Key Productivity Principles

It is not enough to be busy, so are the ants. The question is: What are we busy about?

> – HENRY DAVID THOREAU

THOSE WITHOUT GOALS like to complain about being bored. They're always looking for another distraction.

Those with goals try not to complain at all, but when they do, it's that there's not enough time in the day. They're always looking for another ten minutes.

That's what will happen with you as a goal achiever, if it hasn't happened already. You'll have too many exciting projects going on at any one time to ever be bored. You'll also begrudge time-wasters, while becoming more frugal with your hours and always looking for ways to stretch them. If there were coupons for extra time, you'd clip them.

I don't have time-coupons, but here are four of the best principles I know of for maximizing your efficiency each day: *The 80/20 Rule, Kaizen, The Compound Effect*, and *Avoiding BSOS*.

THE 80/20 RULE

The 80/20 Rule, also known as the Paetro Principle after Italian economist Vilfredo Paetro, says that twenty percent of activities account for eighty percent of results. By way of example, in the business world *The 80/20 Rule* plays out like this:

- 20% of customers account for 80% of sales.
- 20% of customers account for 80% of returns and complaints.
- 20% of products account for 80% of revenue.
- 20% of the employees produce 80% of the results.
- 80% of the productivity happens during 20% of the day.

We can use *The 80/20 Rule* as a test for determining where we may be wasting time, and where best to invest our time.

Ask questions like:

Assuming 80% of my productivity happens during 20% of the day, what hours am I most productive?
Consider working on your most important goals during these peak productivity times.

What 20% of tasks account for 80% of progress on my goal?
Focus on those tasks before anything else.

If 20% of my time-wasting activities account for 80% of my procrastination, what can I do to reign those activities in?
Make playing video games a reward for meeting daily goals rather than a distraction. Earn it.

What 20% of activities bring me the most joy?
Ask yourself how you can make more time for these.

What 20% of things trigger 80% of my anxiety?
How can you eliminate or reduce them from your life?

What 20% of people in my life cause 80% of my stress?
Maybe it's time to set firm boundaries.

What 20% of people in my life make me happiest?
Maybe it's time to invest more time in these relationships.

What 20% of food is responsible for packing on most of my pounds?
What are some healthier go-to alternatives?

What 20% of exercises do I actually enjoy?
Try one of these and see if it's easier to stick with your exercise goal.

What 20% of discretionary spending accounts for 80% of waste?
Maybe it's time to start investing instead of squandering.

Think about *The 80/20 Rule* when planning your months, weeks, and days. Be on the lookout for that outcome-driving 20%, and you'll soon begin seeing it everywhere.

KAIZEN

Kaizen is a Japanese term describing a philosophy of continual improvement in efficiency and outcomes. As organizational theorists Masaaki Imai describes it, "The *Kaizen* philosophy assumes that our way of life—be it our working life, our social life, or our home life—deserves to be constantly improved."

Practicing *Kaizen* is a way of thinking and seeing. Here are some ways to begin thinking and seeing *Kaizen* now.

Strive To Improve

This is the essence of *Kaizen*. Strive every single day to do a bit better, be a bit more skillful, accomplish a bit more, or go a little further towards achieving your goals than you did the day before.

By focusing on gradual improvement, *Kaizen* invites you to be gentle and steady here. No extreme demands on yourself. No harsh judgements. Like the slow dripping of water that eventually wears down the stone, *Kaizen* is immensely patient but effective.

There's a time and a place for massive action on our goals, and then there's a time and a place for the slow and steady pace of *Kaizen*. Which approach is best depends on you and the nature of the goal. But as a rule of thumb, big goals require massive action at the beginning and around certain important milestones, while *Kaizen* sustains progress between these higher-effort points.

Pass Through Setbacks With Ease

If yesterday everything that could go wrong did go wrong and it set you back three weeks on achieving an important goal, it would be only natural for you to feel discouraged. You may be tempted to give because now any progress you make over the coming days won't feel like progress at all—It will just feel like "catching up" to where you had been before the setback.

By grounding focus back to today from yesterday and from yesterday to today, *Kaizen* remedies this problem. You can let go of concern over how far behind you've fallen, and you can stop stressing about "catching up" to where you were. **Your only intention today is to improve on yesterday.** And, lo and behold—since yesterday sucked, that won't be hard to do!

The results?

First, you get to skip beating yourself up and feeling miserable.

Second, freed from those negative emotional drags, you end up getting back on track and overcoming the setback with greater ease and speed than you would have otherwise.

Find The Balance

There's a story about the Buddha having a sudden insight into life and enlightenment. He's sitting by a river when a boat floats slowly by, carrying a music teacher and his pupils. The Buddha hears the teacher say, "If the string is too tight, it will snap. If the string is too loose, it will not play."

The Buddha realized then that achieving enlightenment required a middle way between laxity and austerity. You can't be undisciplined, but you can't take self-discipline to an extreme either. (Have you noticed this middle-way theme weaved throughout this book in different ways?)

This is also the message of *Kaizen*. If you're too ambitious today, you'll snap under the self-imposed pressure. If you aren't ambitious enough today, you'll accomplish little or nothing.

We know this from experience, don't we? We get sick of being overweight and out of shape couch potatoes and so suddenly decide we're going to run five miles every day this week. Then two blocks into day one we feel like death and decide to turn around and head home. *Snap* goes the string of ambition. Our aim was unrealistically high, so the next six days find us back on that couch, bag of chips in hand, exercise goals on hold indefinitely. String of ambition too loose to play.

Practicing *Kaizen* is more about how you see things than what you do. There's a Zen to *Kaizen* that helps you emotionally detach from outcomes while becoming more engaged and effective in the work that produces those outcomes.

Try thinking in terms of *Kaizen* for a few weeks, and you'll see what I mean.

THE COMPOUND EFFECT

Where *Kaizen* may be thought of as a philosophy, *The Compound Effect* is evidence that the philosophy works. And impressive evidence at that.

The Compound Effect says that small efforts made consistently produce tremendous results over time. In his appropriately titled book *The Compound Effect*, Dan Hardy simplifies the idea with the following equation:

Small Choices + Consistency + Time = Significant Results.

It's a powerful concept, and we know it's true.

Example: If you changed nothing else in your diet and give up your two cans of Coke Classic a day habit, in one year you'll have lost almost 30 pounds. A small choice. Taken daily for a year. Outsized outcome.

An important thing to remember about *The Compound Effect* is that it can take a while to notice big changes. For most of the time, results may seem insignificant. But invisibly, just beneath the surface of our consistent efforts, the magic of compounding is working. Finally, the day comes that those significant results seem to "happen all at once."

To see what I mean, think of doubling one cent every day for thirty days . . .

At the end of the first week, you only have $0.64

By day fourteen, you're up to $81.92

At this point, it seems like we're starting to see some of that compounding magic because the next day, mid-month, your one cent has grown to $163.84.

But the magic hasn't broken a sweat. It just keeps going.

By day 20 . . . $5242.88

By day 25, you've broken six figures . . . $166,772.16.

Day 28, you've crossed into the millionaires' club . . .

$1,342,177.25.

And just two days later, day 30, you've reached $5,368,709.12.

All from a single compounded cent.

The critical thing to notice is that it's not until those last three days of the month that the big magic happens. Remember this when you have been working for weeks to grow a positive new habit, or achieve an ambitious goal, but don't seem to be getting the results you hoped for.

Be patient. Stick with it.

Remind yourself that *The Compound Effect* is working, and huge results are inevitable if you don't give up.

BEWARE BSOS

Stay on target . . . Stay on target.
— GOLD 5 TO GOLD LEADER

As you begin achieving more and more goals, you will grow in confidence and ambition. Ideas for new goals and projects will come to you with increasing frequency. In fact, don't be surprised if you're jolted out of sleep some nights with grand inspirations.

This is good because goals are good. Expanded vision is good. Inspiration is good. But if you're not careful, you may keep jumping from "good" goal to "better" goal to "even better" goal, without finishing any goals at all. It's called *Bright Shiny Object Syndrome* (*BSOS*), and you must beware of it.

Here's the rule of thumb: **The bigger your goal, the slower you should be to suddenly ditch it for a new goal.**

Sometimes dropping once-important goals that no longer serve you and replacing them with better goals is the right thing to do. Lives, circumstances, and priorities change. But this should only ever be done with cool and thoughtful deliberation.

The best time to reconsider your priorities and shift goal gears is when you're doing your monthly or yearly reviews. Rarely should you ditch a major goal on a whim, or even during weekly or daily reviews. After all, if a flirtatious new goal is all that important, then it can probably handle waiting until the end of the month or year while you follow through on the current commitments you've made to yourself.

With experience, you'll learn to recognize *BSOS* when it happens. A new and inspiring goal will land in your lap and purr for your attention, but you'll be able to smile at it, give it a nice pat on the head, then set it aside so you can get back to work.

You can honor your current goals while also honoring those inspirations by using your *Dreamlist* to capture them for future review.

Alternately, you can create an *Idea Bucket List* where you put ideas that you'll review at the end of the month and then decide if any or all should be added to your *Dreamlist* or become new goals right away.

* * *

With *The 80/20 Rule, Kaizen, The Compound Effect,* and inoculation against *BSOS,* your relationship with the calendar and clock will change for the better. As well as one can master time, you will master it. And while there will rarely ever be "enough time in the day" to achieve all of your goals, you will no longer go to bed frazzled over your incompletes. Instead, you'll wake up excited about them. You'll no longer be at war with the clock. You'll be in healthy competition with it. It's a far better, more effective, and more enjoyable way to live.

CHAPTER 28

Be Here Now

May you live all the days of your life.

— JONATHAN SWIFT

THERE IS A PARADOX we must embrace if we hope to be both effective and happy goal achievers. It's this: While working to unfold our ideal future, we must also stay grounded in the here and now. This day, this hour, this moment. We must be here now.

The motto "be here now" was popularized by Psychologist turned mystic Ram Dass in his book by the same title. It is once a statement of fact and a gentle imperative.

It's a statement of fact for the simple reason that now is the only place we can be. The past and the present forever converge in the eternal moment.

It's a gentle imperative because our monkey minds are frantic little buggers. They're constantly leaping from past memories to imagined futures and back again while never settling down in the here and now.

But it's precisely here and now that we do the work of moving beyond our past to create a better future. It's by being present that we skillfully navigate today and stay on the path to that bright and promising tomorrow.

So how, pray tell, do we stay grounded in the present while also focused on the future? Well, there is no simple, clear-cut answer. I did say this was a "paradox," after all. But by learning to sit with this paradox we become more effective goal achievers, and happier goal achievers.

The goal planning method you learned in *Part 3* embraces the paradox by encouraging you to telescope your goal focus from year, to month, to week, to today. So just following that method will help reconcile the need to be forward-thinking while grounded in the present. Here are two more ideas that will help, too.

FILE AWAY YOUR WORRY

As Jesus said, "Give no thought of the morrow, for sufficient to the day is the evil thereof." Sage advice. When working on your goals, file away your worry about the future until the future.

I don't need to concern myself with, let alone worry about, potential obstacles to the success of this book, for example. I don't need to think one bit about building an amazing website on which to sell it, or how to run Facebook ads to promote it, or what to do if it flops and no one wants to read it.

Those are future goals, concerns, and possible obstacles. They can wait.

Today I'm doing today. Now I'm doing now.

I'm writing this draft, this page, this paragraph, this line. Sufficient unto my day is the goal thereof.

A beautiful thing about leaving your worries about future goals in the future where they belong is that many will vanish by the time you get there. Where you imagined mountain-sized obstacles, you'll often find easily manageable molehills.

Remember that, like everything else in life, challenges and obstacles can only show up one day at a time. By worrying about future challenges, you're worrying over an illusion, a no-thing.

So don't.

File away your worry and be here now.

PRACTICE KARMA YOGA

For the spiritually inclined I recommend the practice of Karma Yoga. Karma means action and the effect of action. Yoga refers to union with God or, if you prefer, the Divine Self. So, Karma Yoga can be understood as union with God through work. As the *Bhagavad Gita* puts it:

> *By performing his own work, one worships the Creator who dwells in every creature. Such worship brings that person to fulfillment.* (18:47)

Though called by different names, Karma Yoga is found in every major religious tradition. To practice Karma Yoga, make your work an offering or gift to God by acknowledging that the results belong entirely to Him. This offering can be made as a prayer to God, through the thoughtful surrender of attachment to outcomes, or both.

This isn't about giving up our goals or our vision for the future, being passive fatalists, or asking God to do our work for us. *"Ora et labora,"* said St. Benedict. Pray and work. Our work is our prayer, our prayer is our work. The only question is whether or not we are being aware in it and skillful at it.

Karma Yoga is the practice of being aware and skillful. It's about sanctifying today's work, today.

It's about freeing ourselves from anxiety about the future by recognizing that, ultimately, the results of our work don't belong to us.

And it's about tempering the stubborn pride—important as that is to achieving our goals—with a dose of humility. The joyous humility of recognizing that life and our very ability to have goals at all is a precious gift that we did not earn.

By practicing Karma Yoga, we focus on being here, now. More, since it simply wouldn't do to be ingrates and give God a crappy gift, Karma Yoga reminds us to do our best work, here and now.

CHAPTER 29

Persist And Persevere

Nothing in this world can take the place of persistence. Talent will not: nothing is more common than unsuccessful men with talent. Genius will not; unrewarded genius is almost a proverb. Education will not: the world is full of educated derelicts. Persistence and determination alone are omnipotent.

— CALVIN COOLIDGE

GOAL ACHIEVERS ARE STUBBORN SOBs. We have to be because we're fighting a war on two fronts. There's the outer battlefield of obstacles, setbacks, shortage of time, deficits of money, doubting friends, dubious family, and distractions tempting us away from our goals at every turn. Worse is the inner battlefield. Here that dread foe Resistance mercilessly bombards us with self-doubt, self-recrimination, shame, regret, guilt, anxiety, depression, deception, and anything else it can throw at us. Is it any wonder that we are sometimes tempted to raise the white flag? Resistance can leave us shell-shocked.

247

But once we've reached the rock bottom of *Have Been* and set our sights on the heights of *Will Be*, surrender is no longer an option. A temptation, sure, but not an option. This isn't a fight for some list of goals we'd like to achieve, after all. It's all-out war for the lives we're determined to live. So when times are tough, we hold the line, we persevere, we persist.

Sometimes it's that kind of persistence made of a Willpower crammed full of gutsy synonyms like tenacity, stubbornness, doggedness, resilience, relentlessness. The bold and ballsy kind of persistence that answers obstacles the way Hannibal answered his generals when they told him crossing the Alps was impossible: "We will either find a way or make one!"

Or it can be the kind of persistence tenuously knitted together by frayed strings of faith and called *perseverance*. As Albert Camus rightly said, "Sometimes, carrying on, just carrying on, is the superhuman achievement." Like the divorcee picking up the pieces, the entrepreneur starting over, the aspiring musician practicing stubborn chords, the novice writer writing one more page, the addict abstaining one more day, the inventor going back to that drawing board one more time.

And sometimes—often, even—persistence and perseverance means just showing up and doing the damn work, however tedious it is, and however exhausted we are. As Newt Gingrich said, "Perseverance is the hard work you do after you get tired of doing the hard work you already did,"

HOW TO PERSEVERE

However much you prepare for challenges (that's good), you can never be fully prepared (that's life). And even if you use every tool I've already shared, you will still face times of trial, uncertainty, and doubt. So I want to conclude *Part 4* with some encouragement.

When your resolve is sorely tested, and you doubt your capacity to persist and persevere . . .

Remember Your Resilience

Review your *Victory List* while paying special attention to those victories that came just after the point where defeat seemed certain, or you were close to giving up. These are testaments to your resilience and innate capacity to persevere. Just remembering that you've been there before—in situations where seemingly certain failure turned to stunning success—may be just what you need to steady your nerves and steel your resolve to push on.

Remember That Failure Isn't Final

"What we call failure is not the falling down," said Mary Pickford, "but the staying down." Ponder this. Repeat it. Internalize it. Make it an article of faith.

When setbacks happen it can knock the wind out of us, leaving us stunned and feeling hopeless. It's precisely then that we need to remember that a setback is just a setback, and losing a battle doesn't mean losing the war.

Only two things have the power to keep you from getting back up after being knocked down: 1. Death. 2. Yourself. You can't do anything about death, but **you have** total control over whether or not you accept failure as final.

Fail Fast

Failure is like fertilizer. It stinks to be sure, but it makes things grow faster in the future.

– DENIS WAITLEY

When you fail, don't spend too much time nursing your wounds, cursing the Fates, or feeling sorry for yourself. Objects at rest tend to stay at rest. When that object is you after a setback, it may want to stay at rest on the couch in pajamas eating Doritos, watching Netflix, and feeling sorry for itself. While understandable, it's not a recipe for success or happiness.

There's nothing wrong with taking some mental and emotional recovery time when needed. But limit it to a day or two—a week tops—and then get back to doing the important work of creating your best you and your breakthrough life.

Fail Forward

"Every failure brings with it the seed of an equivalent opportunity," said Napoleon Hill. When you experience a failure, look for that hidden opportunity. You may have to dig for it, but it's always there. If you don't find an obvious one, look for the lesson. Lessons are opportunities in long-form.

If you can't even find a lesson, here's one: If you're running a race and you trip, at least you know you're tripping in the right direction. Forward. Even if you fall flat on your face, you're closer to the finish line than before you fell. As long as you get back in the race, you are always failing forward.

And here's another one: Failure challenges you to push beyond it. By pushing beyond it, you exercise perseverance. Thus, every failure is an equivalent opportunity to grow in Willpower and resilience.

Call On Your Allies

Call on your allies when your courage flags and you don't know if you have any more fight left in you. Share your fears and doubts with someone you trust.

Stubborn individualists like me have a hard time with this. So too those more tender souls who don't like to burden others with their problems. If either of these describe you, remember the famous line from John Donne: "No man is an island, entire of itself; every man is a piece of the Continent, a part of the main."

Remember this when you doubt yourself, your goals, and your future. When confidence flags, call on a goal buddy, mentor, coach, or supportive loved one. Let their confidence in you renew your confidence in yourself. Let their faith in your dreams restore your own faith.

Pray

Urge all of your men to pray, not alone in church, but everywhere. Pray when driving. Pray when fighting. Pray alone. Pray with others. Pray by night and pray by day. Pray for the cessation of immoderate rains, for good weather for Battle. Pray for the defeat of our wicked enemy whose banner is injustice and whose good is oppression. Pray for victory. Pray for our Army, and Pray for Peace. We must march together, all out for God.

– GEORGE PATTON

The older I've gotten, the more I rely on prayer, and the more faith I have in faith. Perseverance, after all, is an act of faith. And prayer—a language of faith—infuses us with hope when we feel hopeless and power when we feel powerless. It steadies us, renews our courage, it helps us again find our way when we've lost our way.

How prayer works, why it works, if there's a God behind it, or if it's all psychological . . . That's for you to decide for yourself. What matters in context of this book about goals is that prayer and perseverance go hand in hand. When your resolve to succeed is sorely tried, try turning to prayer to discover a sustaining strength beyond your own.

* * *

Perseverance demands so little yet so much. Little, because it boils down to just one single decision every single time: *Keep going.* Much, because sometimes just making the decision to keep going takes Herculean strength and courage. Nevertheless, it's always within our power. Which is probably why Victor Hugo called it "the secret of all triumphs."

So welcome the hardships that test your metal. Resolve to persist through trial, and persevere through setbacks. If you do, your success is certain, your victory is assured.

Part 4 Takeaways

No one saves us but ourselves. No one can and no one may. We ourselves must walk the path.

— BUDDHA

1. Know that Resistance is your greatest enemy on the path to achieving your goals. Here are some of the most common manifestations of Resistance:

- Procrastination
- Relying on "feeling like it" before working on your goals.
- *Bright Shiny Object Syndrome*
- Entitlement
- Blame-gaming
- King Baby
- Should
- But
- Can't

2. Remember that goals don't care about your feelings. Don't wait on motivation to do what needs to be done. Take action irrespective of your feelings. This will not only increase your Willpower and integrity over time, but it will

253

often create the feeling you were waiting for. Action creates motivation.

3. Where there's a Will there's a why. Find your why for each major goal so that when you're tempted to give up, you'll be better equipped to stay the course.

4. Change your mind(s). You become what you think about most of the time. Reason with your **critical mind** to convince it that your goals are rational and attainable. Use affirmations, visualization, and guided hypnosis to change your **subconscious mind** about what you are capable of and what is possible in life.

5. Frame goals and failures positively. Frame goals positively, and reframe your perceived failures to emphasize their role as learning experiences and steps on the path of success. You didn't fail, you learned, you practiced, and now you'll improve because of that.

6. Grade and gamify your goals. Celebrate your wins. Sustained effort on your goals can be exhausting sometimes. But there's no reason we can't make it a fun kind of exhausting.

7. Success lives just outside of your Comfort zone, so strive to expand that Comfort zone just a little bit more each day.

8. Feel the fear and do it anyway. Fear is just a feeling and not in itself a reason to avoid taking action on your goals or changing your life for the better. Plus, most of the time you'll find that the fear was unfounded.

9. Declutter your life, starting with these four key areas:

- Your **environment**, so you can work on your goals with clarity and focus.

- Your info **inputs**, because you become what you think about most of the time.

- Your **relationships**. Set boundaries on the drama queens in your life.

- Your **responsibilities**. Be clear on the difference between real and imagined responsibilities, and choose wisely.

10. Create rules, rituals, and systems around similar or related goals to maximize your efficiency and effectiveness each day.

11. Create a vision board or vision journal to communicate your desires to your subconscious mind and help keep you inspired. Look at it for a few minutes every day while evoking feelings of expectancy and gratitude.

12. Find allies. Having goal buddies, mentors, or a success coach is great for keeping you motivated and on track. It can also be great fun to talk about your goals with others who are success-oriented.

13. Be a possibility thinker:

- ✓ Act as if it was impossible to fail.

- ✓ When facing a challenge, instead of saying "I can't," ask "how can I?"

- ✓ Be open and experimental. Embrace *Beginners Mind*.

✓ Ask yourself if there's a better way, make your best decision, then take action.

14. If you're unsure what to do with your life or what your goals should be, experiment with options, play with goals, and **prototype** your breakthrough life.

15. Remember the four key productivity principles:

✓ *The 80/20 Rule,* which says that 80% of results come from 20% of activities.

✓ *Kaizen*, which counsels gradual improvement, day by day.

✓ *The Compound Effect*, which promises outsize results if you follow *Kaizen*.

✓ Avoid *Bright Shiny Object Syndrome (BSOS).*

16. Remember that the journey matters as much as the destination. **Enjoy the trip. Be Here Now by filing away tomorrow's worries and practicing Karma Yoga.**

17. Decide that you will persist and persevere through any challenges to achieve your goals. If you do this, success is assured.

Remember:
✓ You are resilient.

✓ Failure isn't final.

✓ When you fail, fail fast.

✓ When you fail, fail forward.

✓ When struggling, call on your allies for support.

✓ When struggling *and* when succeeding, call on divine support. *Pray.*

Conclusion

*The greater danger for most of us is not that our aim is too high
and we miss it, but that it is too low and we reach it.*

— MICHELANGELO

ONGRATULATIONS! You now have everything
you need to achieve your goals and create a life of
victory and accomplishment—a breakthrough life.
Here are three final tips and some concluding thoughts.

DON'T MARRY YOUR PLAN

*For every failure, there's an alternative course of action. You just
have to find it. When you come to a roadblock, take a detour.*

— MARY KAY ASH

Never forget that every part of your plan is a means to
an end.

That end is success.

The means are negotiable.

If you can skip a step to achieve the desired end, skip it.
If you can find an easier way to achieve your goal, do it. If
nothing goes according to plan, replan.

And keep replanning as many times as it takes.

There is always a way to achieve your goal, and your job is to find it. So don't allow setbacks and detours to upset or dissuade you. Remember that they are just part of the process.

TAKE SUSTAINED ACTION

By thought the thing you want is brought to you; by action you receive it.

— WALLACE D WATTLES

Take action, however small, on at least one of your breakthrough goals every day.

Well, almost every day. We are told that even God gave himself a day off, so you probably should too. And then there are *Fuck-it* days—which I now suspect God may also use, if 2020 was any indicator.

Other than those obvious exceptions, strive to take a step every day towards creating your breakthrough life, even if it's just a baby step.

Working on your goals every day helps sustain your momentum. And if you take a step every day in the direction of your goals, it's only a matter of time before you achieve them and have the breakthrough life of your dreams.

BE WILLING TO PAY THE PRICE

Nothing ever comes to one that is worth having except as a result of hard work.

— BOOKER T. WASHINGTON

By using this goal planning method and the success tools I've shared, I promise you will succeed.

Will your victories come quickly and easily?

Sometimes yes.

Sometimes no.

But they will come.

If you stick with it. If you cultivate the tenacity and determination required to diligently work the goal plan you've created. And if you're willing to pay the price. The price is sometimes steep—in time, energy, sweat, tears, even money. But the return on that investment is always far greater than the upfront costs. The return is a new life of greater freedom, accomplishment, and happiness.

Which brings me to my final, final point and my adieu . . . Your goal plan is an incredibly useful tool, but its greatest benefit isn't in the goals it will help you achieve, *but in the person it will help you become.*

As you develop a goal-oriented consciousness, you gain greater clarity of purpose, self-discipline, and self-respect. You will grow in integrity by keeping your self-covenants and achieving those things you promised yourself you'd achieve.

You'll be a more successful person, yes.

But more, you'll be a happier person. You'll be a better person. And that's saying a lot, because you're already pretty great in my book.

I wish you fantastic success and abundant joy on your journey!

Resources 1

Example Planner Pages

For visual learners, here are some example goal planning pages that you can refer to while creating your own plan. I use my own *Breakthrough Goals! Planner* for these examples, but you can adapt the method for any planner you choose, or even just use your goal journal.

DREAMLIST

🏃 **MY BREAKTHROGH DREAMLIST**

───┤ HEALTH/FITNESS ├──────────────────────────────

☐ LOSE 30 LBS

☐ DO 100 PUSHUPS

☐ JOIN A GYM

☐ START INTERMITTENT FAST

☐ LEARN YOGA

☐ HIRE PERSONAL TRAINER

☐ HAVE MY IDEAL BODY

ONE-YEAR PLAN

MY BREAKTHROGH YEAR

> 2021

BREAKTHROUGH GOALS THIS YEAR | **DOMAIN** | **GRADE**

1. Lose 30 Lbs — HEALTH/FITNESS
2. Launch My Own Business — CAREER/VOCATION
3. Pay Off Credit Cards In Full — WEALTH/PROSP.

HEALTH/FITNESS
- [ ] Start+Follow Weight Watchers
- [ ] Walk/Exercise 240/365 Days
- [ ] Get 24 Hr Fitness Membership
- [ ] Be Able To Do 25 Pushups
- [ ] Intermittent Fast For 30+ Days

RELATIONSHIPS
- [ ]
- [ ]
- [ ]
- [ ]
- [ ]

CAREER/VOCATION
- [ ] Write+Publish Goal Guide
- [ ] Incorporate Biz/LLC
- [ ] Build/Launch Website
- [ ]
- [ ]

SPIRITUALITY
- [ ]
- [ ]
- [ ]
- [ ]
- [ ]

WEALTH/PROSPERITY
- [ ] Set Up Budget On Mint.com
- [ ] Save $100 Emergency Fund
- [ ] Save $500 Emergency Fund
- [ ] Save $1000 Emergency Fu
- [ ]

PERSONAL DEVELOPMENT
- [ ]
- [ ]
- [ ]
- [ ]
- [ ]

FUN/STUFF
- [ ]
- [ ]
- [ ]
- [ ]

MONTH PLAN

🦋 MY BREAKTHROGH MONTH

MONTH/YEAR

FEB 2021

BREAKTHROUGH GOALS THIS MONTH

	Goal	DOMAIN	GRADE
1	INCORPORATE BIZ/LLC	CAREER/VOCATION	
2	LOSE 4+ LBS	HEALTH/FITNESS	
3	FINISH GOAL GUIDE 1ST DRAFT	CAREER/VOCATION	

HEALTH/FITNESS
1. FOLLOW WT. WTCHRS. 20/30 DAYS
2. WALK/EXERCISE 20/30 DAYS
3. RESEARCH YOGA
4. _____
5. _____

RELATIONSHIPS
1. CALL MOM WEEKLY
2. HAVE GOAL MEETUP W/GARY
3. DO 'DREAM PARTNER' TRAIT EXERCISE
4. _____
5. _____

CAREER/VOCATION
1. BRAINSTORM/CHOOSE BIZ NAME
2. BUY GOALREBEL.COM
3. SET UP SOCIAL MEDIA ACCOUNTS
4. WRITE OR EDIT 20/30 DAYS
5. DESIGN BIZ LOGO

SPIRITUALITY
1. MEDITATE OR JAPA 20/30 DAYS
2. RE-READ THE BHAGAVAD GITA
3. RE-READ GOSPEL OF JOHN
4. MORNING PRAYER 20/30 DAYS
5. EVENING PRAYER 20/30 DAYS

WEALTH/PROSPERITY
1. PAY OFF DISCOVER BALANCE
2. PAY $100+ ON CAP 1 BALANCE
3. SAVE $100 IN EMERGENCY FUND
4. SET UP MINT.COM BUDGET
5. RESEARCH SIDE-HUSTLES

CREATIVITY
1. MAKE 1 COLLAGE
2. DO 1 DRAWING
3. READ BOOK OF TENNYSON POEMS
4. HAVE 2+ 'ARTIST DATES'
5. _____

PERSONAL DEVELOPMENT
1. DO AFFIRMATIONS 20/30 DAYS
2. DO VISUALIZATIONS 20/30 DAYS
3. READ 'THINK + GROW RICH'
4. READ 'ATLAS SHRUGGED'
5. CREATE A NEW VISIONBOARD

FUN/STUFF
1. PLAY D+D!
2. VISIT THE MUSEUM
3. BUY NEW PF FLIERS
4. _____
5. _____

WEEK PLAN

🏃 MY BREAKTHROGH WEEK

8TH TO **14TH**   MONTH/YEAR: **FEB 2021**

BREAKTHROUGH GOALS THIS WEEK

	Goal	DOMAIN	GRADE
1	BRAINSTORM+CHOOSE BIZ NAME	CAREER/VOCATION	
2	FOLLOW WT. WTCHRS. 5/7 DAYS	HEALTH/FITNESS	
3	WRITE/EDIT 5/7 DAYS	CAREER/VOCATION	

HEALTH/FITNESS
1. WALK/EXERCISE 5/7 DAYS
2. INTERMITTENT FAST 5/7 DAYS
3. SCHEDULE DENTIST APPOINTMENT
4. BUY BOOK ON YOGA
5.

RELATIONSHIPS
1. CALL MOM
2. HAVE GOAL MEETUP W/GARY
3.
4.
5.

CAREER/VOCATION
1. BUY GOALREBEL.COM
2. REVIEW LOGO ARTISTS ON FIVERR
3.
4.
5.

SPIRITUALITY
1. MEDITATE OR JAP[...]
2. MORNING PRAYER [...]
3. EVENING PRAYE[...]
4.
5.

WEALTH/PROSPERITY
1. SAVE $50 IN EMERGENCY FUND
2. MAKE $100 DISCOVER PAYMENT
3. MAKE $100 CAP 1 PAYMENT
4. ADD $100 TO ACORNS ACCOUNT
5. RESEARCH HOME OWNERSHIP STEPS

CREATIVITY
1.
2.
3.
4.
5.

PERSONAL DEVELOPMENT
1. DO AFFIRMATIONS 5/7 DAYS
2. DO VISUALIZATIONS 5/7 DAYS
3. READ 'THINK + GROW RICH'
4. COLLECT VISION BOARD IMAGES
5.

FUN/STUFF
1.
2.
3.
4.
5.

DAY PLAN

MY BREAKTHROGH DAY

[X] Tu We Th Fr Sa Su

DATE: **03/10/21**

AFFIRMATION/INTENTION

I'M A HIGHLY MOTIVATED, HIGHLY
DISCIPLINED GOAL ACHIEVER!

GRADE

✓ TODAY'S GOALS

BREAKTHROUGH GOALS

1. DO MY DAILY DISCIPLINES
2. WRITE/EDIT FOR 2 HRS.
3. GOAL MEETUP W/GARY

SECONDARY GOALS

4. SCHEDULE DENTIST APPT.
5. MAINTAIN INTERMITTENT FAST
6. ORDER YOGA BOOK
7.
8.

TERTIARY GOALS/TASKS

- [ ] CLEAN BATHROOM
- [ ] READ 1 CH 'ATLAS SHRUGGED'
- [ ] START VISION BOARD
- [x] MAKE DISCOVER PAYMENT
- [ ] LOOK UP MUSEUM HOURS
- [ ]
- [ ]
- [ ]

DISCIPLINES/HABITS

- ● PLANNING
- ● AFFIRMATIONS
- ○ VISUALIZATION
- ● JOURNALING
- ○ MEDITATION/JAPA
- ○ UPLIFT READING
- ● MORNING PRAYER
- ○ EVENING PRAYER
- ○ EXERCISE/WALK

🕐 TODAY'S SCHEDULE

5:00
6:00 ✗
7:00   SPIRIT + PD
8:00
9:00
10:00 VOCATION
11:00
12:00
1:00   HEALTH/FIT

2:00   MEETUP
3:00
4:00   FLEX
5:00
6:00   SPIRIT + PD
7:00
8:00
9:00   FLEX
10:00

NOTES:

SINCE MY SPIRITUAL AND PERSONAL DEVELOPMENT GOALS OFTEN OVERLAP, I LIKE TO USE THE SAME COLOR FOR BOTH AND I USUALLY TIME-BLOCK THEM TOGETHER TOO. MY POINT . . . FEEL FREE TO ADAPT THE PLANNING METHOD TO FIT _YOU._

PROJECT PLAN

**BREAKTHROUGH
PROJECT PLANNING**

COMPLETE	PROJECT	DOMAIN
☐	**LAUNCH BLOG**	**CAREER/VOCATION**

SUBSTEPS/NOTES

M1 CHOOSE/BUY DOMAIN+HOSTING
☐ BRAINSTORM+CHOOSE DOMAIN NAME   HOSTGATOR
☐ BUY DOMAIN NAME   GODADDY **?**
☐ RESEARCH + BUY HOSTING   SITEGROUND
☐
☐

M2 DESIGN SITE
☐ CHOOSE+INSTALL WORDPRESS THEME
☐ CREATE CORE PAGES   ⟶   ◯ BLOG PAGE   ◯ CONTACT PAGE
☐   ◯ ABOUT PAGE   ◯ FAQ
☐
☐
☐

M3 LAUNCH!
☐ PRE-WRITE 6 POSTS   ⟶   ◯ POST 1 ◯ POST 4
☐ SET UP SOCIAL MEDIA ACCOUNTS   ◯ POST 2 ◯ POST 5
☐   ◯ POST 3 ◯
☐
☐
☐

M4
☐
☐
☐
☐
☐

Resources 2

Goal Achiever Resources

BREAKTHROUGH GOALS! PLANNER PAGES

Download your free *Breakthrough Goals!* Planner and other goodies here:

www. breakthroughstrong.com/op/free-goal-planner

OTHER GOAL PLANNERS

There's a plethora of goal planners on the market today so I've only included my (current) top three. Whether you choose one of these, or another, here's two tips to consider.

Tip 1: Use A 90-Day Planner

Three-month planners give you greater flexibility for modifying your plan throughout the year. A less tangible, but I think still valuable, benefit is that there's a joy and renewed excitement for achieving goals that comes with buying a new planner. With a ninety-day goal planner you get to experience this four times a year, rather than just once a year.

Tip 2: Experiment

Try different planners on for size until you find the best fit. That's part of the fun too!

Clever Fox Goal Achievers Planner

This is the highest quality planner on this list in terms of product materials and overall design. It's a 90-day planner.

Favorite Features

- ✓ Planning pages with mind maps for top 5 goals.
- ✓ Weekly tracking box for 8 habits.
- ✓ Weekly review sections, including progress grading (Though it's based on how you feel about the week, not a grade or a number).
- ✓ Daily quotes.
- ✓ High quality design.

Get Stuff Done Planner

This is tied with the Clever Fox for as my favorite goal planner. It has slightly lower paper quality than the Clever Fox, but it's also more affordable. It too is a 90-day planner.

Favorite Features

- ✓ Planning pages for 4 top goals.
- ✓ Two page spread for making a vision board.
- ✓ Weekly review pages, with next week planning for four projects.
- ✓ 1-10 scoring for each day.
- ✓ Helpful division of goals into top 3 Focus Goals (i.e., breakthrough goals), Important, Immediate, and Other Tasks.
- ✓ Great price.

Law Of Attraction Planner

This is a fun and in-depth planner that comes in twelve month and three-month versions (I've used both). I don't recommend it if you're new to goal planning, but it's worth considering if you want to try something new, or if you're inclined to focus on your feelings and emotions in relation to the Law Of Attraction.

Favorite Features

✓ Extremely in depth and long-term goal planning at start of planner, including an "Awareness and Self-Discovery" exercise, Mission and Vision Statement pages, Life Statement page, foldout vision board page, mind maps, and more.
✓ Daily review questions.
✓ Top 3 monthly goals, with "Action Steps."

ONLINE COMMUNITY

Join my new online community that includes a *Breakthrough Goals Course* based on this book, and other personal-growth courses too!

- Courses.breakthroughstrong.com

BOOKS

Here's a list of some of my favorite personal development books and other resources.

Health & Fitness

- *The Sedona Method,* by Hale Dwoskin.

- *The 4-Hour Body: An Uncommon Guide to Rapid Fat Loss, Incredible Sex and Becoming Superhuman*, by Tim Ferris.
- *No Sweat: How The Simple Science of Motivation Can Bring You A Lifetime Of Fitness*, by Michelle Segar.
- *Feeling Good: The New Mood Therapy*, by Dr. David Burns.

Wealth

- *Rich Dad Poor Dad*, by Robert Kiyosaki
- *Cashflow Quadrant*, by Robert Kiyosaki
- *Money: Master The Game*, by Tony Robbins
- *Think And Grow Rich*, by Napoleon Hill.
- *Total Money Makeover*, by Dave Ramsey
- *Manifestation Miracle:*
  destinymiracle.com/r/ganesha47/home

Vocation

- *The 4 Hour Work Week*, by Tim Ferris.
- *Tools Of Titans*, by Tim Ferris
- *Dotcom Secrets*, by Russel Brunson
- *Free To Focus*, by Michael Hyatt.
- *Principles: Life and Work*, by Ray Dalio.
- *Do The Work*, by Steven Pressfield.

Personal Development

- *Success Principles*, by Jack Canfield.
- *Psycho Cybernetics*, by Maxwell Maltz.
- *See You At The Top!* By Zig Ziglar.
- *The Power Of Your Subconscious Mind*, by Joseph Murphy.
- *As A Man Thinketh*, by James Allen.

- *7 Habits Of Highly Effective People*, by Stephen Covey.
- *The Compound Effect*, by Darren Hardy.
- *Maximum Achievement*, by Brian Tracy.
- *Designing Your Life*, by Bill Burnett and Dave Evans.

Relationships

- *How To Win Friends & Influence People*, by Dale Carnegie.

Spirituality

- *The Bhagavad Gita*
- *The Holy Bible*
- *Autobiography Of A Yogi*, by Paramahansa Yogananda.
- *The Journey Within*, by Radhanath Swami.
- *Everyday Zen*, by Charlotte J. Beck.
- *The Oversoul & Compensation* (essays), by Ralph Waldo Emerson.
- *Be Here Now*, by Ram Dass.

Creative

- *The Artist's Way*, by Julia Cameron.
- *Drawing On The Right Side Of The Brain*, by Betty Edwards.
- *Making Comics*, by Lynda Barry.
- *If You Want To Write*, by Brenda Euland.
- *Big Magic*, by Elizabeth Gilbert.
- *The War Of Art*, by Steven Pressfield.

Fun/Stuff

- *Dungeons & Dragons 5th Ed.*

A REQUEST

If you found value in this book, would you take a moment now to leave a quick review on Amazon? It would sure make my day, and earn you some good goal karma, too. Thank you in advance!

I'd also love to hear about your goals and any feedback on the book that you'd like to share. You can contact me at goalguyak@akspencer.com.

ABOUT THE AUTHOR

A.K. Spencer is a writer, artist, and entrepreneur with a zeal for helping others achieve their goals. His writing on goal achievement is noted for its nonconformist GenX sensibilities and for encouraging a playful balance between no-excuses self-reliance and open-hearted creativity.

He has a B.A. in Social Sciences and an M.A. in Literature and Writing. Rumor has it that he is planning a daring escape from Portland, Oregon.

Connect With A.K.

You can find links to all of A.K.'s social media and other sites in one handy place: **Linktr.ee\goalguyak**.

Made in United States
Orlando, FL
15 December 2023

41002352R00157